Three Steps to Quantum Wealth:
The Wealth Heiress' Guide
to *Financial Freedom* by Investing
in Cryptocurrencies

(Or How a Little Money Can Grow into Crazy Wealth)

Linda P. Jones

Three Steps to Quantum Wealth:

The Wealth Heiress' Guide to *Financial Freedom* by Investing in Cryptocurrencies

ISBN-13: 978-1-990476-00-6

Published by: Expert Author Press
https://www.expertauthorpress.com/

Canadian Address:
1908 – 1251 Cardero Street, Vancouver, BC, Canada, V6G 2H9
Phone: (604) 941-3041
info@expertauthorpress.com

Table *of* Contents

Section Four: Staying Wealthy in the Quantum Age

Acknowledgments

Many thanks go to my publisher, Bob Burnham, and his administrative assistant, Stella Mariz Nadela; my talented editor, Kathy Palokoff; proofreader Ruth Thaler-Carter; and graphic designer Frances Louw for your hard work making this book possible. I couldn't have done it without you!

To my awesome sisters, Marilyn and Susan (and brother-in-law Jim), and friends Barb, Sharon, Rachel, Jaci, Jamie, Rosie and BJ. You are all amazing women in your own right.

To my wonderful clients in the *Be Wealthy & Smart VIP Experience.* Thank you for your confidence in me and for having me as your wealth mentor.

And finally, I want to thank YOU for inspiring me to write this book for all future Wealth Heiresses and Heirs.

Your Wealth Heiress/Heir is the smart, confident, successful, and wealthy person already inside of you who has yet to be fully discovered.

How to Read This Book

This is a book about how to attain financial freedom. As we enter into a technological revolution, you have the option to invest in early-stage opportunities that were not accessable by everyday investors before. Within the bigger picture of how wealth is created, you will see that by adding a small investment in cryptocurrencies to your portfolio, it is possible to get a head start on the massive wave of money coming, billions invested by institutions, and possibly benefit from some extraordinarily high compounding rates.

It was written in mid-2021, in the midst of a relatively early and evolving time in this new technology. I have included information and some opinions that are relevant to this moment, while anticipating future regulations and laws. The world we are living in is incredibly dynamic, and things are changing daily, so over time, as things evolve, I encourage you to stay updated on new perspectives, technology and uses for digital assets that emerge in the future.

This book was written for multiple audiences across generations and with different knowledge levels. I have divided it into four sections that I recommend reading in order. Each section begins with a quote to set the tone for that section.

The first section is about the innovations of the Quantum Age and why I am so excited about the wealth-building the future will bring. The second section is important investing principles that are life-changing. The third section is about the Three Steps to Quantum Wealth and why your financial freedom is possible faster than ever. The fourth section is about how to maintain your wealth and not lose it. Although the predominant investing vehicle, or money engine, I am showing you is cryptocurrency, this is not a book to teach you everything about cryptocurrency. It is an introduction to digital assets meant for everyday investors, many of whom have no idea what is about to happen in FinTech. I felt the book would be incomplete if it did not cover additional important information necessary for your wealth-building, so you are well-prepared and ready for what is about to change your life, whether you invest in it or not.

Each chapter begins with a quote by me to capture a key thought in the chapter, and ends with a summary (The Bottom Line), as well as questions or exercises to help you use the ideas and concepts (Leap into the Quantum Age). There are several valuable tools in the back of the book. The Additional Resources show you how to get more information and stay updated. The Key Word Glossary (which I hope you refer to often) is to help you understand new terminology the Quantum Age brings.

Enjoy, and welcome to the astounding possibilities of wealth-building in the Quantum Age.

Section One

You Can Create Wealth with Digital Assets Faster and Easier than Ever

"The financial industry is transforming to a digital economy, and we see digital assets as one of the most significant forces impacting our industry over the next five years."

— Ron O'Hanley, Chair and CEO, State Street Corporation, with $40 trillion of assets under custody

Chapter 1

Building Wealth in the Quantum Age

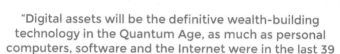

"Digital assets will be the definitive wealth-building technology in the Quantum Age, as much as personal computers, software and the Internet were in the last 39 years."

The Quantum Age is what I call the next technological revolution that humanity is about to experience. It is bigger than just one new technology — like the Internet — and much broader in scope. We are about to see a technological leap encompassing transportation, health care, energy, technology, communications and finance. You will recognize it by noticing new inventions such as electric vehicles, robotics, flying cars, high-speed trains, consumer space travel, green energy, virtual reality, genomics, quantum computers, decentralized finance, blockchain and digital assets, including cryptocurrencies.

Some people call this technological age "Web 3.0" or the "Fourth Industrial Revolution," but it involves much broader advances in technology than just on the web. It is not just an industrial revolution; it is also a financial revolution that some people call financial technology or FinTech.

As you will see, leaps in technology cause massive wealth creation. My intention is to help you understand what is happening and know how to invest for financial freedom, so you can benefit from it instead of missing out or perhaps only realizing the amazing wealth creation happening in hindsight.

Technology and Wealth Creation

Looking forward and trying to predict the future can be difficult, but we can use our experience in the past to help us. During our lifetimes, massive wealth has been created every time technology takes a leap. Let's review the last 30 years to understand how wealth exploded when computers and the internet came on the scene and these major new technologies created incredible investing opportunities.

For example, as an investor, you might have missed the wealth-building significance of IBM inventors Mark Dean and Philip Don Estrange, whose research team invented a computer that IBM released for sale in August of 1981, which rapidly grew to $15 billion in sales. In the next decades, Apple, Hewlett Packard, Dell and other tech companies made billions of dollars creating personal computers (PCs). After starting his laptop business in his college dorm room, Michael Dell made a $40 billion fortune. In 1985, Microsoft introduced a PC operating system and software that eventually made it the most valuable company in the world, minting 12,000 millionaires and three billionaires along the way. New technology creates massive wealth.

Researchers introduced the Internet in the 1960s and '70s, but it was scientist Tim Berners-Lee who created the World Wide Web (WWW) protocol in 1989 that enabled email, instant messaging, video chat, discussion forums, social media and online shopping. In 1994, Amazon created an online shopping website for books, then expanded into other areas and created $1 trillion of wealth in a shopping category that didn't exist before. Along the same line, although small-scale electric cars have been around since the 1800s, it was Elon Musk who created a quantum-age luxury electric vehicle and in 2021, became the wealthiest person on the planet, with $197 billion net worth and Tesla stock valued at $773 billion.

You can see how each time a new category of technology is invented, it is a massive new wealth-creation opportunity. Yet, you might not hear about it or consider investing in it until years later. Or you may have missed out on the opportunity altogether and been kicking yourself. Or you have a friend who became rich investing in a new technology, even though they can't find their way out of a paper bag. It is only obvious to the masses in hindsight; while technology booms happen, the press is often downplaying the trend. Yet it is undeniable that massive wealth is created when new technology is invented that advances us to the next level of modernization. Somewhat quietly, trillions of dollars of new market value in technology companies and cryptocurrencies are underway, but you might have only heard about bitcoin, which, as you will learn, is not a technology I would invest in. More about that later.

New technology, and especially new categories of technology, creates trillions of dollars worth of wealth, yet even though we might use this technology, we can miss out as investors. How much could your investment portfolio have benefited from technologies you probably use but might not have known to invest in? If you used AOL, Microsoft, Google, Facebook, Apple and Amazon and did not invest in them, it is not your fault. No one told you how big these companies were going to get and how much wealth they would create. If you missed some of these amazing investment opportunities, though, it is not too late, because an even better investing opportunity is on the horizon and I'm going to tell you all about it.

Large Amounts of Money are Flowing into Cryptocurrencies

Early internet and crypto entrepreneurs, the Winklevoss twins, received money after settling a Facebook lawsuit for $65 million and parlayed it into bitcoin to become the first crypto billionaires in 2017 and today are worth $3 billion each. In 2021, nine new billionaires who made their wealth in bitcoin and other cryptocurrencies were added to the *Forbes List of Billionaires,* with another four returning from the previous year.

We are starting to hear about large institutions investing in cryptocurrencies; Square, MicroStrategy and Tesla are putting bitcoin on their balance sheets. Cathie Wood added cryptos worth $820 million to her ARK Innovation fund. The nation's oldest bank, BNY Mellon, is building crypto products to invest in. More than 80 central banks are reportedly studying and testing central bank digital currencies. Germany just passed a law that institutional funds such as pension funds and insurers (currently managing over $2 trillion) can hold up to 20% in cryptocurrencies. But even with all of this happening, the wave of money investing in cryptocurrencies is still in its infancy.

Taking Advantage of the Opportunity

The cryptocurrency market has grown to $2 trillion alone and could be headed to $10 trillion (and probably much more) in a few years. While this is underway, no one tapped you on the shoulder, took you by the hand and said, "Pay attention and invest in this; it will create wealth for you."

Until now.

From the single mother who got divorced and started with almost nothing and was able to grow it into a six-figure nest egg by investing in cryptocurrency, to the young man who lived at home and became a multi-millionaire by buying a cryptocurrency on his phone app because Elon Musk tweeted about it, to the teenager who invested her "stimmy" (stimulus) check into crypto and made a cool $500k — the stories are incredible, unlike anything I have ever experienced with investing.

Some people seem to be "lucky" to find wealth. For others, it is very hard. We have all been told we have to work hard and that only through hard work will we succeed. You might think you have to work at a job, put in long hours and be exhausted to earn a living. If you are financially successful, you can save enough for a down payment on a home and buy a car, but then you have to go to your job every day to pay the mortgage and car loan. You are tied to a job and maybe even a career for the money so you can pay your bills, take care of yourself and your family, and have a nice life.

It may not be work you enjoy doing. Do you have a choice? It doesn't feel like you do. That is why so many people crave financial freedom: so they don't have to go to a job they hate, work for a boss they loathe and spend their life chained to a reality they didn't feel like they chose. However, please understand: *If you invest well, it can change all of that and bring you financial freedom.* This is not only because you can make a lot of money with cryptocurrencies, but also because FinTech is changing the very definition of money and banking.

In the future, cryptocurrencies will give you opportunities for multiple streams of passive income such as the opportunity to be your own bank and earn interest on loans to others. The new technology interest rates you can earn with cryptocurrencies today aren't what you are offered on a savings account in a bank (about 0.5%), but rather 4% APY (Annual Percentage Yield). Even earning 10% APY rates are possible today, without taking a lot of risk.

Although the topic of all the emerging technologies in the Quantum Age is intriguing, for our purposes, we will focus mostly on cryptocurrencies (virtual currencies that have value and can be exchanged for value), decentralized finance (no central bank or financial company in charge) and blockchain (a computerized record of transactions). I have selected these areas because they are easy to invest in, require a small amount of capital and are compounding at the highest rates I have ever seen as an investor.

Let's start by defining cryptocurrency in the context of blockchain and decentralized finance. *"A cryptocurrency (or crypto currency) is a digital currency that works as a medium of exchange on distributed ledger technology, typically a blockchain, which gives each transaction a unique and unhackable record. It is nearly impossible to counterfeit or double-spend. It is not centrally controlled like our paper currency is today, it is decentralized and in limited supply where the amount in existence can only be changed by a vote of the holders of the cryptocurrency. It does not exist in physical form, only on computers or phones. It is an enormous change and benefit that cryptocurrencies use decentralised control as opposed to centralised digital currency and central banking systems."*[1]

---

[1] Wikipedia.

Closing the Wealth Gap

Consider this the most important book about how to make and keep wealth that you have ever read. I can say that with confidence because I know where we have been and where we are going.

We have been living in a world with stock indexes that average about 8% to 10% annually, and now we are going to a world of parabolic growth of new technologies that I believe will grow at much faster rates. This means you will be able to compound your money at higher rates than ever before, dramatically shortening the time it takes to build wealth. If you pay attention, you will learn how to grow what you have into six or seven figures and beyond, and how some people had the opportunity to grow money into eight or nine figures. *I will show you it is possible to cut as much as a decade off the time it takes to reach your financial goals.*

You are about to learn something that only a small handful of high-net-worth investors who have researched and invested in future technology know. They understand how our world is about to change in the most profound way because we are entering the Quantum Age. They are not going to tell you exactly how and where to invest to benefit from this knowledge.

But I will.

The Queen of Compounding Speaks

As a wealth mentor and self-proclaimed Queen of Compounding, I identify where compounding rates may be the highest, so you know the best places to invest your money. I'm not a financial advisor. I don't invest your money for you. Rather, I show you where you may be able to compound your money at the highest rate for the longest period possible.

How do I do that? By identifying trends of high long-term growth rates.

This is not a "get rich quick" scheme. That would be like buying a lottery ticket and getting rich overnight. No, it is not that quick, but I will show you how you may compound your money at potentially higher rates that may grow your wealth and get you to financial freedom faster than your current path.

I will show you what and how much to incorporate into a traditional investment portfolio. You will have enough information to be able to manage your money by yourself, without paying Wall Street thousands of dollars in fees each year. I will share research with you, but it is up to you to decide if it is something that makes sense for you to invest in given financial circumstances, such as the size of your portfolio, age and risk tolerance. I am going to show you what I believe are the cryptocurrencies that have the most potential for wealth-building. It is up to you to decide what to do with the information. Ultimately, this is about you and your future wealth.

My background is more than 25 years in the investing field. I am not a technology person; I'm a financial person. The way I describe things may not be technically perfect, so to the tech experts out there, please understand that I am trying to explain a complicated subject in lay terms to everyday investors, not to tech experts. This is more about getting the investment angle correct than getting the exact tech angle. I am trying to simplify a complex subject like computer coding without making readers have to learn how to code. I may speak in generalities and skip over something that a tech expert might think is important, but in the grand scheme of investing may not be, so please allow me some slack if my tech description is not perfect. Rest assured that my investment advice is on point.

You will learn my formula for Three Steps to Quantum Wealth, because the potential for wealth-building is truly that massive. With cryptocurrencies, the time (T) in years to invest is dramatically shortened and the compounding rates (c) are incredibly high, which means you need very little money (M) to invest and possibly create exponential wealth. The amount of money already created by these investments is staggering.

And you will learn how not to make the same mistakes as most people who acquire a lot of wealth relatively quickly. That is called "sudden wealth syndrome" and it results in 70% of people spending, losing or otherwise being without all of their newfound wealth in about five years. To make sure that doesn't happen to you, I will give you Five Steps to Maintaining Your Wealth.

Next, I am going to share more about why crypto-currencies are like early-stage businesses and how our ability to invest in them early is part of the secret to their high compounding rates of return.

The Bottom Line

This is a remarkable time of opportunity where everyday investors can find financial freedom through the innovations of the Quantum Age. Now is the time to get started early and act upon your knowledge in the tsunami of wealth coming from innovation.

Leap into the Quantum Age

To take your own leap into this exciting era, open your mind to the possibility of earning much higher rates of return on your money.

Chapter 2

Digital Assets Will Bring Enormous Wealth

"Digital assets are growing so fast; it is shaving decades off of traditional investing timelines."

Early-stage businesses traditionally have been very good investment opportunities that compound money at high rates, which I call powerful "money engines." Traditionally, these newer businesses were invested in by Venture Capitalists (VCs), multi-millionaires that provided private equity to fast growing businesses that did not have access to capital markets. They invest in new ventures, either business start ups or young businesses because the returns are superior, beyond anything the everyday investor can earn. *"According to the National Bureau of Economic Research, the average return is 25 percent."*[2] At an average annual return of 25 percent, your money will consistently double in under every three years and 10x in a little over 10 years. For everyday investors, private equity investments have been out of reach and you have been conditioned to average annual returns in a 1% to 10% range of possibility.

Low compounding rates are what keep you from becoming wealthy. People don't build wealth by keeping their money in a savings account earning less than 1%, yet many people do just that. To become wealthy, you need *high rates of compounding.* This is something the wealthy know very well, yet the everyday investor usually does not. This book can help you reach the higher rates of compounding, but first you have to understand where money compounds at high rates.

---

[2] Kevin Johnston, *Finance.Zacks.com website,* https://finance.zacks.com/return-venture-capitalists-expect-10600.html

Early-Stage Businesses Compound at High Rates

Now we will look at the list of *Inc. 5,000 Fastest Growing Companies*. The median (half grew faster and half grew slower) growth rate for private companies on the list in 2020 was 165%. Just to give you an idea how high some compounding rates of businesses can get, the companies in the top 10 on the list grew 48,337%; 46,800%; 40,899%; 26,011%; 25,359%; 20,485%; 17,922%; 16,396%; 15,072% and 13,876% averaged over three years. The 100th-fastest-growing company grew 3,473% and the 5,000th company grew 55%. These are all privately held businesses with at least $2 million in revenue. Because they are private companies, you don't have the chance to invest in them. However, if you could and if your money grew 48,337%, a $1,000 investment would grow to $483,370. We will come back to this in a minute.

As everyday investors, we tend to think of money engines that compound money as stocks, bonds, precious metals or real estate, and the spectrum of compounding rates of return available to us is typically under 10%. A tech stock like Apple or Google might get us to 20% returns or above for a period of time. Rarely do we hear about investments that provide consistently higher rates of compounding, such as a triple-digit return, for any consistent length of time.

Everyone knows that Warren Buffet became one of the wealthiest people in the world and one of the investing greats by investing in stocks. Few realize his Berkshire Hathaway stock returns were about 22% annually. At that rate, it would take you decades to create substantial wealth, versus the people who started businesses and had astounding thousands of percent returns. For example, it would take you 31 years to grow $1,000 invested at 22% to $475,504, while our example of the $1,000 investment in the *Inc. 5,000 Fastest Growing Company* achieved that in three years, saving 28 years of investing. Truly, being able to get high rates of return creates substantial wealth quickly.

We are so conditioned to think lower rates of compounding are "safe" and that it is good to get rich "slowly." Meanwhile, Wall Street is seeking out every high return they can and building a wall around them so only high-net-worth investors can invest in them. I have shown you that to build wealth, you must compound at high rates and that business owners can do that. That is probably why more than 47% of millionaires are business owners.

Consistent high compounding rates are required for someone to become a billionaire. For example, Peter Thiel invested $1,700 into PayPal in 1999 (in a venture capital investment) and it grew to $5 billion in 2021, which is more than 96% compounded annually for 22 years.

The difference between private equity and venture capital is private equity is capital invested in a company or other entity that is not publicly listed or traded on a stock exchange. Venture capital is funding given to start-ups or other young businesses that show potential for long-term growth. Wealthy people invest venture capital in young businesses at low valuations that can grow at thousands of percent rates of return, eventually going public and selling shares on the stock exchange. That is one way they build significant wealth.

But again, to be a venture capitalist or invest in private equity, you have to be an "accredited investor," which means you must have an income of more than $200,000 a year (or $300,000 if you share a joint income). If you are not making that much, you can still be considered an accredited investor if your net worth, not including your primary residence, exceeds $1 million. In addition, you often have to invest at least six figures in each deal. That rules it out for a lot of people, especially people who are in more of a wealth-building phase rather than those who already have more than a million dollars and usually much more than that.

Everyday investors haven't had access to investment options that can compound at such high rates. Theoretically, having to qualify as an accredited investor is necessary to "protect" you from riskier investments, but it is also keeping you from earning higher returns. *However, now, because of cryptocurrencies, you can invest small amounts of money and achieve enormous rates of return that were previously inaccessible to you.* That is what is so exciting about the Quantum Age.

Cryptocurrencies are Compounding at the Highest Rates in History

What makes cryptocurrency investing so unique is that you have the ability to invest early, almost like a venture capitalist. As you may already know, bitcoin compounded at 200% per year for 12 years, which meant $1,000 invested for five years grew to $243,000. But few people know it is not just bitcoin that is rising dramatically. Check out these five-year returns on other cryptocurrencies:

- Polkadot was worth $2.93 in 2017 and grew to $20.95, up *615%*.

- Uniswap launched in 2020 and by June 2021, it was worth $24.60, a gain of *5,025%*.

- Cardano's ADA token in 2017 was $0.02 and in June 2021, its price was $1.50, an increase of *7,400%*.

- XRP was worth $0.006 in 2017 and in June 2021, reached $0.92, a gain of *15,233%*.

- Dogecoin was $0.0002 in 2017 and by June 2021, was at $0.32, a gain of *159,900%*.

- Binance Coin was $0.10 and by June 2021, had risen to more than $350, a gain of almost *350,000%*.[3]

Another example of spectacular five-year returns is Ethereum, the second-largest cryptocurrency by market capitalization after bitcoin. It is a decentralized blockchain that supports its native coin ETH, thousands of other cryptocurrencies and NFTs (non-fungible tokens). Its growth has been astounding: In the last five years, one ETH went from $7.10 in 2016 to $2,144, an increase of about *30,000%*.

Again, *these are five-year returns.* It is so foreign for stock market investors to see returns like this, but believe me, the

---

[3] *Forbes.com*

hedge funds are noticing. Hedge funds are professional money managers for accredited investors. They can employ different strategies and earn a percentage of profit plus annual fees. Hedge funds will go wherever they can make the most money so they can keep a percentage of it. It seems like a new hedge fund announces their entry into cryptocurrency investing every day. They understand the power of compounding money at high rates.

When the wave of Wall Street money (hedge funds, endowments, family offices, institutions, etc.) really starts to come into cryptocurrency, I think it is going to grow exponentially. That is why I say digital assets, of which cryptocurrency is one example, are very undervalued right now. The first inning of the Quantum Age innovation has barely begun.

Even One-Year Returns are Spectacular for Some Cryptocurrencies

It is not just five-year returns that are spectacular. Some cryptocurrencies start their value below a penny, and you can buy them for $0.00000000001 when they are created. That is why some of the returns on cryptocurrencies are in the thousands of percent even in one year, such as 5,990%; 9,388%; 18,526%; 21,138%; even 30,574%. *These are actual 1-year returns* on some cryptocurrencies.

In 2017, the cryptocurrency XRP increased in value by *31,000%:* It climbed from $0.006 to $2, according to CoinMarketCap. That means a $1,000 investment in XRP grew to $310,000. Bitcoin grew "slower" during the same year, increasing 1,762% where a $1,000 investment grew to $17,620. Still incredible.

When we look at returns for the largest cryptocurrencies by market cap for *the last one year through September 2021, the average compounding rates are in the thousands of percent.* These are actual one-year compounding rates for the top 10 cryptocurrencies (excluding stablecoins that stay steady at $1 value) as displayed on CoinPaprika.com: Bitcoin, *342%;* Ethereum, *814%;* Hex, *14,858%;* Cardano, *2,663%;* Binance coin, *1,432%;* XRP *355%;* Solana, *5,171%;* Dogecoin, *8,696%;* Polkadot, *600%;* Terra, *12,166%.*

That is a one-year average return of 4,709% per cryptocurrency, or $1,000 invested grew to $47,090. These are returns that normally would take decades to earn in the stock market. Cryptocurrencies, or what some call the "blockchain asset class," are incredible investment opportunities that are saving you years of investing in slower compounding money engines like stocks.

As quoted on Intechopen.com (with their own bold emphasis): "Cryptocurrency returns have averaged a **level equal to roughly 20 or more times those of** conventional currencies or equity investment. Although cryptocurrencies offer the attraction of enormously high returns, cryptocurrency investment is also accompanied by substantially higher risk."[4] We will address how to minimize risk later in the book. I still believe we are very early in this investment and although the returns are spectacular (20 times better than stocks), they have only just begun.

Let me give you an example how cryptocurrencies are able to save you decades of time of investing in other money engines. Janie started investing for retirement late in life. At 47, she finally started putting money away. Fortunately, she invested a small amount in a cryptocurrency. It was priced below a penny at $0.0003. Before long, she had turned her $2,000 investment into $547,000. That is what investing in cryptocurrencies can do for you because they have such high rates of compounding. It doesn't take much money to grow a small amount into a very nice amount. Talk about an opportunity to close the wealth gap.

This is a very transitional time where we are moving into the Quantum Age and making a lot of changes because of COVID-19. The pandemic has changed many things. Some peoples' finances have been devastated. Others weathered it okay. The pandemic advanced the rate of technology adoption by about 10 years, because more people had to move online, use

---

[4] Intechopen.com.

Zoom, go to telemedicine and so forth. New technology is being boosted by more people moving online. More people moving online means more adoption of the technology, which means it becomes more mainstream. This is a pivotal time for digital assets that are about to become commonplace.

Now you understand why I am so excited for you. While most investments that reach extremely high rates of compounding are restricted to accredited investors who are already wealthy, *cryptocurrency is basically like investing in early-stage businesses*, but does not require you to already have $1 million of investable assets or $100,000 to invest in each deal. The spectacular rates of return we will talk about are mind-boggling and can be life-changing for you, even if you only invest a small amount.

The Bottom Line

It is all about compounding, and there has never been a time in our history where compounding opportunities are so available. Why? Cryptocurrencies are in a fast-growing technological revolution.

Leap into the Quantum Age

There are times in history when technology leaps forward and a lot of wealth is created.

1. Can you name a time you experienced or a time in history when a natural resource, asset or invention gained tremendous value?

2. Who benefited?

Chapter 3
Digital Assets are Money Engines for Wealth

"Add a money engine like a cryptocurrency that has a consistently high growth rate to your portfolio and watch your wealth accumulate faster than you believe is possible."

In the first chapter, I argued that new technologies create wealth through compounding opportunities that didn't exist before. This is an opportunity to make money if you are aware of the trends while they are happening. In the second chapter, you saw how early-stage investments compound your money at higher rates than stocks. Compounding (c) your money well saves you from having to invest more money or wait more years to reach your goal. It is the most important factor in my *Wealth Building Formula (McT)™*. In fact, once you understand its importance, you will understand why Wall Street cares about getting a high compounding rate and not about getting rich slowly. As Albert Einstein said, *"Compounding is the eighth wonder of the world. He who understands it, earns it; he who doesn't, pays it."*[5] Indeed, the "c" is the mightiest factor of my McT formula.

The importance of earning high rates of compound interest became clear to me when I was investing in Internet and technology stocks in the 1990s. These tech companies were compounding at rates we had not seen before, and many were compounding at over 100% per year. One of my stock investments, America Online, was a company whose services would be similar to a combination of Gmail and Yahoo today. It was a fast compounder during the last technological revolution. Compounding at high rates means a small amount of money can grow into a fortune quickly. A $1,000 investment in AOL when

---

[5] *Quora,* https://www.quora.com/Albert-Einstein-famously-stated-"Compound-interest-is-the-eighth-wonder-of the-world-He-who-understands-it-earns-it-he-who-doesn't-pays-it-"-"-How-the-average-person-use-this.

the company went public on March 19, 1992, would have appreciated to $147,446 in 1998. This is rare because the company had already gone public, so to continue at an astonishingly high compounding rate for a stock was unusual at the time. Yet it taught me that compounding at a high rate would bring wealth quickly. It was one stock of many that resulted in doubling my $1 million portfolio to $2 million in 1 year.

Today, I believe if you add a money engine like a cryptocurrency that has a consistently high growth rate to your portfolio, you will watch your wealth accumulate faster than you believe is possible. But before we talk about which cryptocurrencies to invest in, I want you to understand why your mindset and mentors are crucial factors for wealth-building success and attaining and maintaining financial freedom.

The Six Steps to Wealth

When I was investing and compounding my first million dollars, I discovered something life-changing: A progression of action steps had to happen to create wealth. I call them the *Six Steps to Wealth,* and they are:

1. Create a Wealthy Mindset

2. Save a Nest Egg

3. Find a Mentor

4. Invest in a Money Engine

5. Compound at a High Rate

6. Protect Your Wealth

When you look at Step 4, you will recognize the term "money engine" and in Step 5 "compound at a high rate." We have already talked about the importance of these in wealth-building, but I wanted to show them in the context of all six steps. As you will see, by investing in cryptocurrencies as our money engine and being able to compound at high rates, we will be able to compress the Six Steps into *Three Steps to Quantum Wealth.* We will go into depth on that and the other steps later so you have all of the tools you need for wealth-building.

28

As I have been sharing with you, the formula I developed to explain the components of the compounding step is the *Wealth Building Formula (McT)™*. This formula includes three factors: Money (M), compounding (c) and Time in years (T). The only reason compounding is a small "c" is to give it a catchy way to remember the formula "McT," not because the "c" is less important. In this book, you are not only going to see how high compounding rates shorten the time for wealth creation, but also how to maintain your wealth, which for many people, seems to be a bigger problem than creating it in the first place.

Wealth Creation is Speeding Up

As you may know, Apple is now the most valuable company on the planet, worth more than $2 trillion. Apple became a trillion-dollar company in 42 years, Microsoft became worth a trillion dollars in 44 years and Amazon became worth a trillion dollars in 24 years. Google became a trillion-dollar company in 22 years. Then came bitcoin, which grew to $1 trillion faster than any investment in history: It took only 12 years. *The time it takes to become wealthy is speeding up because of the high compounding rates of digital assets, which are saving you a decade of wealth-building time (in years) to create wealth, the "T" in my Wealth Building Formula (McT)™.*

As you saw in the last chapter, compounding rates in cryptocurrencies are much greater than in stocks. Let's compare. If you invested $1,000 in Apple, it would have grown to $4,799 in five years, or in XRP cryptocurrency, it would have grown to $373,220. If Apple continued at the same rate, it would take *77.7 years* for it to be worth $373,220, so once again, you see crypto is making you wealthy a lot sooner!

In 2021, the largest S & P 500 stocks by market capitalization after Apple are: Alphabet, Amazon, Microsoft and Facebook. They are all technology companies. Their combined market capitalization is $8.472 trillion. The total market cap of all 2,603 listed stocks on U.S. stock markets is $45 trillion, so these five companies make up 18.6% of all of the stock market's wealth. Before these five companies were founded and went public, the $8.472 trillion level didn't exist.[6]

What if each of them created their own cryptocurrency to spend on their websites? Facebook is said to be creating its own called "Diem." Amazon and Microsoft would be wise to create their own cryptocurrencies. The city of Miami is creating one. If they did create their own cryptocurrencies, how many people would use them? Wouldn't more usage cause their value to increase? How much wealth would each asset create? The possibilities are exciting to imagine.

Wall Street Favors Institutional Investors

In the 1990's, the media did not explain that the Internet would be used by all of us to be more efficient and connect us to people near to us and around the world. We weren't given advance notice by our brokerage firms that the Internet was something you could invest in that could create millions of dollars for you. Maybe your advisor did recommend a technology mutual fund, but it was after the big gains had already been made and they could show you the incredible *past* performance numbers.

That is what happened while I worked at a large Wall Street stock brokerage firm: The firm offered technology funds to institutional investors first. They reaped all the rewards of consistent high returns. Years later, after a five-year track record was established, a "cloned" retail fund was sold to the public. By then, unfortunately for everyday investors, the big gains had already been made and the top of the market was near. Regular people did not benefit like the institutions did.

I see this same thing happening today, and I don't want the everyday investor to get into this investment opportunity late in the game or miss it altogether. Fortunately, we are still early because institutions are just barely beginning to invest in cryptocurrencies. I want you to understand the potential of cryptocurrencies and be invested early, when a modest

---

[6] Market Cap Source: *Companiesmarketcap.com website.*

investment can grow substantially and you can benefit when the huge wave of money from large institutions comes into cryptocurrencies after you already own them.

Financial Media is Often Wrong

Don't expect to hear about great investing opportunities in the financial news media. They may not get investing trends or cycles correct. Back at the peak of the technology boom, around year 2000, the media said Internet companies had no value and no earnings, and that it was foolish to invest in them. They also said the Internet was over-promising, under-delivering, a fad and would be rejected. There was nothing to see here; move on. *This is why you cannot rely on the media and you must do your own investing research or rely on your wealth mentor.*

For example, in December 2000, during the Internet stock frenzy, a ridiculously negative article in the *Daily Mail* reported:

*The **Internet may only be a passing fad for many users,** according to a report. Researchers found that **millions were turning their back on the world wide web,** frustrated by its limitations and unwilling to pay high access charges. They said that email, far from replacing other forms of communication, is adding to an overload of information. Experts from the Virtual Society, which published the report, said **predictions that the Internet would revolutionize the way society works have proved wildly inaccurate.** Many teenagers are using the Internet less now than previously, they conclude, and **the future of online shopping is limited.** Steve Woodgar, director of the society said, "We are often presented with a picture of burgeoning Internet use, but there is evidence already of drop-off and saturation among users. Teenagers' use of the Internet has declined. **They were energized by what you can do on the Net** but they have* *been through all that and then **realized there is more to life in the real world and gone back to it** ... "[7]*

How laughable were their predictions and supposed research now that we can look back 20 years after this silly report? Did millions of people turn their back on the web? No. Did people refuse to pay more for access? No. Was the future of online shopping limited? No. Were teenagers so bored that they abandoned the Internet? Heavens no!

If you relied on the media to forecast the future, you would have missed some of the best investments in our lifetimes, and probably did. Yes, it is true that valuations did get ahead of themselves, and some companies went public that shouldn't have. Who can forget Pets.com going public with zero earnings and then going out of business? That didn't mean that Internet technology wasn't real and there weren't some gems that grew into giants like Amazon and later, Google.

Listening to the media report on price action as a gauge whether or not to invest would also not have served you well. Amazon's stock price per share peaked at $106.70 in 1999, then declined to $5.97 in 2001 before growing to $3,731 in July 2021. If you were only going by the stock price movement, you might have thought that Amazon's stock was a dud. If you were following the growth of the Internet and companies that were dominant, however, you would have been able to hold Amazon through the trough.

What we are hearing today from CNBC, Bloomberg and others is that cryptocurrencies are a joke, a fad and will never be taken seriously as investments. Sound familiar? It starts to make sense that they would discourage investors from taking cryptocurrencies seriously when you understand that banks and financial institutions are losing billions of dollars in deposits to cryptos and they are direct competition. They have to keep their advertisers happy and in business for the news networks to stay in business.

---

[7] James Chapman, *Daily Mail*, December 5, 2000.

The news is selected based on what is best for the news station, not for what is best for your wealth. They are a for-profit business, and they rely on advertisers and ratings. To make money, they sell advertising, mostly to financial companies and pharmaceutical companies nowadays. That means you are likely to receive news that is favorable to those advertisers, yet most people don't put two and two together and see the media biases. They are glaring!

You Now Have a Source of Unbiased Investing Information

This is one of the reasons I wanted to become a wealth mentor. There aren't a lot of business models that provide unbiased financial news. Many media people, whether online, YouTubers or on TV, receive compensation from sponsors to promote them or have a particular viewpoint. I wanted to have a business model where I could be unbiased and share investments that are compounding at the highest rates that will lead to your financial freedom.

There are investment publications that are paid to promote certain investments and are beholden to hedge funds. Some of them are even owned by hedge funds and have recommended you buy stocks that hedge funds are heavily shorting. They draw in new buyers, then hedge funds sell short (sell at a high price to buy back lower later) to drop the price, causing unsuspecting investors to panic and dump their shares, then hedge funds buy shares at a lower price and make big profits. They do this because it is easier for them to make money on a price dropping than to wait for it to rise.

Wall Street is Often Wrong

It wasn't only the media that looked at Internet companies incorrectly in 1999 (and now crypto). Wall Street said companies were to be valued by how many "clicks" they got and how many eyeballs looked at their websites. Brick-and-mortar companies were said to be passé.

What caught my attention as an investor who thinks for herself and does the research was the realization that if you didn't have to invest in office buildings or storefronts, or even pay rent, there was extra money that could go to bottom-line profits. That is what drives stock prices higher. Companies that could create commerce without having to create a physical location, or could dramatically expand online from a few locations, would be more profitable than the businesses that had to pay for locations, rent and employees to staff them.

It is no wonder the venture capitalists that invested early in Internet companies made fortunes. Savvy venture capitalists love to invest in disruptive technology, but that is something everyday investors aren't taught or helped with. The everyday investor might have missed Amazon's gains of 120,000% in 20 years where $10,000 invested in its IPO would have been worth $12 million in 2020.

Wall Street and the media are not always giving us great advice. More research is necessary on our part to determine where to invest and compound our money best. There are even a lot of myths around money that I want to dispel because it is also stopping you from maximizing financial success. In the next chapter, I will review the myths and show you why they do not serve you.

The Bottom Line

Everyday investors have been shut out of getting in on the ground floor of many investments. The Quantum Age and your wealth mentor will change all that. Now you have the opportunity to build wealth and arttain financial freedom in an unprecedented way.

Leap into the Quantum Age

Almost 51% of people say they lack knowledge about cryptocurrencies. To get up to speed quickly (in addition to reading this book), tune in to my free Cryptocurrency Playlist of podcasts at *https://lindapjones.com/podcast-list-cryptocurrencies/*.

Chapter 4
There is No Virtue in Getting Rich Slowly and Other Financial Myths

"On Wall Street, money managers who beat stock index averages are sought after and rewarded with millions of dollars. Money managers who underperform indexes are fired. In other words, they reward getting rich fast, but tell you it is better for you to get rich slowly."

One financial myth we have been told is that getting rich slowly is the best path to wealth. With compounded returns of our digital assets so high, we are told that cryptocurrency "is too risky" or "is a bubble." We are discouraged by bankers, business media and Wall Street for wanting to invest in cryptocurrencies, yet they know the top 1% wealthiest are enthusiastically embracing crypto investments.

The reason they say everyday investors should get rich slowly is because they say the tortoise wins the race over the hare. That is a fictional story, it is not reality and it is certainly not how Wall Street works.

Do you think a professional money manager would survive for even a minute if they managed money in a way that was the slowest? Or earned a sub-par return? Or were getting there slowly instead of beating the S & P 500 index average? Heavens, no! On Wall Street, money managers who beat stock index averages are rewarded with millions and sometimes even billions of dollars, and money managers who underperform are fired. In other words, they believe in getting rich fast, but have sold you a bill of goods for why you have to get rich slowly. Because they outperformed stock indexes in 2020, 15 hedge fund managers made $1 billion or more, compared with only eight the previous year. The top earner, Israel "Izzy" Englander of Millennium Management, earned $3.8 billion.

Why do they tell you that you should be getting rich slowly? And why is the example always given a fictional story of a race between a tortoise and a hare? They can't even quote real numbers to prove their point.

Of course, you don't want to gamble or take too much risk. That is not what I am talking about, but there is no virtue in getting rich slowly. It does not make you holier or closer to God. There is no benefit in taking longer to accumulate money. There just isn't. This idea that somehow getting rich slowly is the ideal is ridiculous and laughable to anyone who makes their living managing money, unless they are trying to convince you that low returns are good for you.

This is just one of many myths that I want to share with you, so you have a clear and unbiased view of the best path to financial freedom, instead of detours presented to you. Here are six additional myths.

Myth #1: You Can Budget Your Way to Wealth

Besides getting rich slowly, another financial myth is that you must budget every penny you spend. There are all kinds of websites, books and podcasts about why you need a budget. Frankly, studies have shown that millionaires don't use budgets, so if using budgets is said to be how they became millionaires, it is false.

Budgets can feel very restrictive, almost like diets. They ultimately give you a bad relationship with money because, like a diet, you want to splurge and go off them as soon as possible. That is why I say that budgets can be hazardous to your wealth.

Rather than a budget, I recommend setting spending priorities. Create your top five priorities where you want your money to go and then make sure you spend, save or invest your money there first. It is a version of the old adage of "paying yourself first," but instead of just putting 10% out of your monthly income into your savings account, you prioritize five places you want your money to go. For example, it can be your 401(k), mortgage, savings, kid's college education fund and a vacation fund. This ensures your money is going to pay for what is most important to you.

The only time I recommend using a budget is if you are on a very tight income. If you don't make much money and are barely able to pay all of your bills, then use a budget to keep track of every penny to make sure you will make ends meet.

Myth #2: Pay off Your Mortgage Early

We live in a time where mortgage money is the cheapest money there is, yet so many people have been convinced that all debt is bad. They work to pay off their mortgage early and pay chunks of money to the bank to get rid of it. They celebrate when their low-interest mortgage is paid off.

I agree that 18% interest on credit card debt is bad. At 18%, debt will double every four years. That is a travesty, especially when the items the debt is used for are probably depreciating in value. However, that is much different from paying 3% interest on a home mortgage. At 3%, the debt will take 24 years to double. Also, the 3% may be tax deductible if you itemize, so you are not really even paying 3% interest.

Let's pretend you own a bank. What behavior would you want people to do? Would you want them to pay low credit card interest first and leave their high-interest credit cards for last? Yes. Would you want them to save money in your bank accounts and earn low interest so you can loan out the money at high rates of interest? Yes. In recessionary times, would you want them to pay their mortgage before they paid other bills, ensuring that you get a larger piece of their paycheck? Yes. In summary, as a bank owner, it would be best for you if people paid off low-interest credit cards first, leaving higher rates for last, saved an emergency fund in a little-to-no interest account, and paid off their mortgage first before other bills because we are in hard times, and you would be sure to get paid. Surprise, surprise: That is the financial advice that is popular today. It is exactly what is best for the bank owner, not for you.

What is best for you is to first pay off your high-interest credit cards. For example, pay off any 18% interest rate cards before 8% interest rate cards. It would also be best for you to invest as much as possible into an investment that would provide you with a high return instead of paying off a 3% interest rate mortgage. When you pay down 3% debt, it is the same as if you earned only 3%.

The real problem I see with paying off your mortgage early (besides earning a low effective rate of return of 3% interest saved vs. 10% growth in the stock market or perhaps even higher in cryptos) is the opportunity cost (OC). When you are paying lump sums of principal or extra payments to pay down your mortgage early, that is money that could have been invested in your retirement fund. Instead, you put it into paying off the mortgage, so now you will have less principal in your retirement fund and less growth on the money that could have been compounding at about 10% annually and doubling every 7.2 years. This has made many people who have paid off their mortgages with early retirement savings poor or not having enough invested in their retirement accounts to be able to retire. They did it because they thought it was good financial advice.

I do agree with making a 1/12 extra payment per year on your mortgage to pay it down faster, but that is cash flow that is fairly minimal, so it does not have a high opportunity cost like lump sums do. For example, if you have a $1,200 a month mortgage and you pay 1/12th extra, that means $1,200 divided by 12 equals $100. If you add $100 a month to your mortgage payment and pay $1,300 a month instead of $1,200 a month, your mortgage length will be shortened by about seven years from 30 years to 23 years. Good job. It is not costing you much to do so and you are not depriving your retirement savings of being funded like you are if you are paying $10,000 chunks into your mortgage to pre-pay it.

If you had the choice of using $50,000 to pay down your 3% mortgage or invest it into your retirement account, with the mortgage, you would save paying some 3% interest. If you could invest it in the stock market and earn a long-term average return of about 10%, over 25 years, the $60,000 would grow to $650,082. See what I mean? Yes, you would have saved some interest, but at 3%, it is about $125,626. By choosing to pay off your mortgage early instead of investing your money in a retirement account or investments for retirement, you have deprived yourself of over half a million dollars. That is a *massive* opportunity cost (OC).

I'm not opposed to eventually paying off your mortgage, I'm only opposed to doing it at the expense of not funding your retirement plan as fully as you could have.

OC is what you could have earned on your money if you invested it elsewhere. A 401(k) is an example of where you could have used the money instead and potentially earned a lot more, perhaps three times more because it is typically the best compounder of your money at about a 10% average per year over the long term.

That is a money engine that is working for you and compounding without any income tax. Your contribution to a traditional 401(k) is also not taxed. If you contribute to a Roth 401(k), you will pay with after-tax dollars, but when you retire, there will not be any income tax to pay. It is important for you to max it out with the most money you are allowed by law because it is such a powerful compounding vehicle for wealth-building.

Whether you invest in a traditional or a Roth 401(k), you are limited to a maximum contribution of $19,500 annually if you are under age 50 and $26,000 if you are age 50 or older. Yes, you can contribute to both, up to a total amount of those limits. If your employer matches part of your contribution, such as the first 3%, you should contribute to that plan to get the full match (free money) from your employer, then contribute the rest up to the maximum amount in the Roth 401(k).

A Roth can be a better choice due to the possible greater tax benefits, especially if you think you will be in a higher tax bracket when you start withdrawing money tax-free after age 59½. Roth 401(k)s also allow you to take penalty-free early distributions in certain special cases and there are no income restrictions such as with Roth IRAs, where if you earn "too much money," you cannot contribute. However, in a Roth 401(k), contributions are not tax-deductible, minimum distributions are required and you must hold your account for five years before you can take tax-free withdrawals after age 59-½. Please consult your tax advisor for more details.

Myth #3: Rent Instead of Buy a Home

There is also a trend of "popular" influencers who have started teaching people not to buy homes, and to rent instead. Companies like Blackrock are buying up the homes, hoping to rent them to you and have you pay the mortgage for them. Not so fast; homes have been one of the best sources of wealth-building for most people. Why? First, because it is a forced savings plan. Every month, you are paying down debt and adding to your principal, getting one step closer to owning your home free and clear.

Second, home appreciation has been tremendous. There is a big wealth disparity between people who own homes and people who rent. Over a 20- or 30-year time horizon, the wealth gap can be millions of dollars difference. The average rate of home appreciation over the long term has averaged about 6%, but it can be much higher in some markets.

Third, you are able to buy an expensive asset on an installment plan. This makes it more affordable, and you even get help from tax deductions if you itemize on your taxes. Don't fall for the "hype" encouraging you to rent. Even after paying for repairs and maintenance, buying, not renting, is the way to go if you want to build wealth and have financial freedom.

Making good financial decisions is not about listening to popular financial gurus. It is about spending as little as possible on the cost to borrow money and making as much as possible when investing money. If you just remember this, you will have financial freedom.

Myth #4: All Debt is Bad

One more thing about debt. The financial gurus are harping on getting rid of debt, but the billionaires are loading up on debt. Once again, there is the dichotomy that what is best for them is not for you. "They" are borrowing five times their stock value and leveraging to buy more. Many hedge funds are leveraging more than 5:1 to build their fortunes and beat the markets. I know that from my days in the investment industry.

I'm not suggesting you use leverage when investing, I'm simply pointing out once again, that what the wealthy are doing is very different from what you are taught to do. They borrow as much as they can as cheaply as possible and try to hedge their risk to invest and become fabulously wealthy; you are taught not to have any debt and to take as little risk as possible so you can "get rich slowly."

The wealthy hedge fund managers are paid for achieving high returns — the highest possible to make their wealthy clients wealthier. They are not of the mindset to get rich slowly. That is how some of them are able to charge fees that pay them $1 billion a year. Of course, sometimes it backfires, and we hear about their disasters, but you would be surprised at how many have quietly and successfully used leverage to invest and create billions of dollars of new wealth.

Myth #5: Avoid Risk

As you can tell, cryptocurrencies are quite volatile. They have to be to get staggering returns on the upside. Along with that comes volatility to the downside. If you don't want volatility, your range of investment choices is going to be quite narrow and the returns will be close to 0% in traditional banking products like an interest-bearing savings account, money market fund or Certificate of Deposit (CD). Rather than avoid risk, a better concept would be to *limit* risk. You can do that by diversifying your portfolio and putting only 3% to 5% into cryptocurrencies. If you are a very aggressive investor, invest no more than 20% into cryptocurrencies. I dedicated an entire chapter about risk and strategies to mitigate it, so I will keep this short for now.

Myth #6: Don't Invest in Early-Stage Businesses that Compound at High Rates

Besides leveraging, money managers are also able to compound at high rates by investing a portion of their funds into venture capital, angel investments and private equity (start-up or early-stage pre-IPO businesses). These are commonplace for institutions, endowments and ultra-high net worth clients. Why not you? The industry response is it is "too risky" for the everyday investor. But these investments generate some of the highest returns available; much higher than stocks, in many cases. What is wrong with investing only 1% to 3% or 5% of your long-term investment capital in a diversified group of them? These are investments that are early-stage, so the compounding rates are much higher than after they have grown large enough to go public and sell shares of stock in initial public offerings (IPOs) on the stock market.

Institutions like Goldman Sachs, JP Morgan and Morgan Stanley have started offering their high-net-worth investors investments in cryptocurrency. Endowments, hedge funds, family offices and other institutions are now investing in cryptocurrency. I think they see the impressive returns and lack of correlation with stocks (meaning they move up and down independently of one another), so it is the perfect complement to a stock portfolio.

High-net-worth investors like family offices, which typically have $50 million or more in investable assets and hire managers and administrators to take care of their financial needs, are typically early investors in successful asset classes. It is like they have their own wealth mentor scouring the planet for the best returns and they invest early (15% of family offices are already invested in cryptocurrencies). The typical brokerage firm gives its richest customers the best-performing investments first. Retail investors with smaller amounts of investable assets are usually offered the investment last, years after institutions and the ultra–high-net-worth investors.

That is why I think if you pay attention to what I am saying now, you can get in almost at a venture capital stage —

before certain cryptocurrencies become the dominant technology and before the wave of big money that I believe will be created in digital assets in the next five years and beyond. What is exciting is you can build your wealth to $1 million beyond the value of your home, so you can become an accredited investor and also invest in venture capital opportunities in the future. Another way to expand your wealth-building, money engines and compounding opportunities.

Again, to be clear, this is for a small portion of your portfolio. I believe you can tolerate volatility in assets when: 1) they have excellent performance numbers long-term, and 2) they are a small percentage of your investment portfolio. I am not suggesting you put all of your money into high-risk assets. Please refer to my asset allocation model in Chapter 9 for suggested investments and percentages in your portfolio.

Where to Earn High Returns without Leverage

The evolving FinTech is more innovative than anything we have seen in our lifetimes and may provide the highest returns we have ever seen as well. If you are a baby boomer, you grew up watching the Jetsons cartoons like I did. We saw them wearing jetpacks, commuting to work in flying cars, talking over video conferencing technology and having robots as maids.

Now we are entering a time when much of the technology in those cartoons may become part of our daily lives. Self-driving trucks, virtual real estate, robot waitresses, genomics, deliveries by drone, digital art and assets tokenized for shared ownership are going to be coming at us fast and furious — much faster than the Internet did. This is a one-time leap that humankind is making in technology and will be a very rewarding time to invest, because each new technology is a completely new market that will create significant wealth.

While we are experiencing a leap in technology in the Quantum Age, many of these technologies require a lot of capital to create the flying car or robot. The great advantage FinTech has is it is created mostly with computer programming, not with steel, rare earth minerals, silver or other commodities (and all of the cryptocurrencies I recommend are "green," meaning they are environmentally friendly). Yes, you need computers to program, but you don't need huge factories to mine cryptocurrencies (again, we are not investing in bitcoin and therefore the mining that bitcoin requires is something we can leave out of our discussion for our investment purposes).

The Bottom Line

Gaining wealth slowly is a myth that can be disastrous to obtaining financial freedom. Now more than ever, you need to take advantage of compounding rates of cryptocurrencies and realize that there is money to be made if you have the right strategy.

Leap into the Quantum Age

What myths do you personally have about getting rich slowly? How have those beliefs served you? After reading this book up to this point, what myths do you feel are changing?

Section Two

Investing Principles for Wealth

"Success in investing doesn't correlate with IQ once you're above the level of 125. Once you have ordinary intelligence, what you need is the temperament to control the urges that get other people into trouble in investing."

– Warren Buffett

Chapter 5
Cryptocurrencies Solve Problems

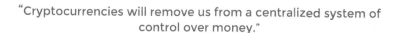

"Cryptocurrencies will remove us from a centralized system of control over money."

When I look at the potential for cryptocurrency, it is hard to put a number on it because cryptocurrencies or digital assets are the way of the future. We are moving from the Internet being a communication device to what Chris Larsen, executive chair, former CEO and co-founder of Ripple, calls "the Internet of value." He aims to make sending money as easy and fast as sending an email. I don't see how this isn't going to happen in the future. To me, it looks like this is the next level of the Internet, and it is even bigger than the Internet because it is going to hold all things of value. Every single thing of value (physical or not) can be tokenized and sent over the Internet. Tokenization is simply dividing an asset into digital pieces that multiple people can invested in.

Any investment that we make in the future could be tokenized. You could invest in a property that gets tokenized and sold as a digital asset to investors, or you could tokenize a Monet painting and people who want to buy a piece of it could buy a tokenized version of the painting. You could divide up a valuable diamond, a vacation condo or a car. Many things will be tokenized so you can invest in them in an affordable way.

In your stock brokerage account, you will have a wallet, and you will have cryptocurrencies as well as tokenized stock. What is a tokenized stock? It represents traditional securities trading on exchanges, but is verified as authentic and cannot be artificially duplicated, such as we see today with synthetic shares of stock sold in dark pools (off exchange, between institutional investors).

Sending Crypto is Fast and Inexpensive

Transferring money with cryptocurrencies can be done in seconds for a cost of less than 3 cents per transaction, and it can be sent worldwide. I remember when the Internet came into being, and people didn't trust shopping online or putting their credit card numbers online. They felt very uneasy about having any of their financial information on the Internet. It was all very uncomfortable at first. There was fraud, but over time, security got better. Now we can't imagine not using the Internet to do all of these things in our daily life: banking, paying bills, making brokerage trades or shopping. We use encrypted technology to make it secure.

Cryptocurrencies are going more mainstream every day. We are seeing the adoption of payment plan providers such as PayPal, Venmo and MoneyGram accepting cryptocurrencies. In the future, I believe all banks are going to give you a secure digital wallet and you will have the ability to own multiple cryptocurrencies.

Not long from now, you will be able to go to the grocery store, bag your items and just walk out without exchanging cash or credit cards. Everything will be automatically calculated and charged to your crypto account on your cellphone. You won't even have to scan items by hand or go through a checkout counter.

Why I Didn't Like Bitcoin

When I first heard about bitcoin, I did not like the fact it was created by an anonymous person or group that sounded like they were promoting anarchy. It felt foreign to learn bitcoins were generated by miners processing transactions and securing the network, required specialized hardware and a lot of energy, and took approximately 10 minutes and 72,000 GW (or 72 terawatts) to mine one bitcoin. *"Bitcoin was set up as a one-computer-one-vote governance system (known as Proof-of-Work) ... Now the Bitcoin network is processed on a huge array of 300-megawatt datacenters."*[8] There was also a huge loss when Mt. Gox, an exchange that sold and stored bitcoin, was hacked. It seemed like bitcoin was fraught with problems.

Eventually, I did a deep dive on research and investigated other cryptocurrencies. I saw that they were leaping forward with new technology, advancing our concept of currency and solving real problems. XRP cryptocurrency caught my attention because it had the ingenious idea to be a bridge currency. That meant it could transfer one type of value to another type with speed and low cost, whether they were other cryptocurrencies, central bank digital currencies (i.e., digital Yuan, Euro, Yen, etc.), or any kind of tokenized value.

XRP could be sent anywhere in the world in a few seconds and cost only a fraction of a cent. Compare that to today when someone from Mexico who works in the U.S. is trying to send money to their family in Mexico. Currently, it costs about 10% for them to do that through a bank or traditional financial institution and can take hours or even days to arrive. In a world where the Internet makes it possible for actions to be instantaneous, it is no longer acceptable for currency exchanges and cross-border transfers to use outdated technology like SWIFT (the Society for Worldwide Interbank Financial Telecommunication) that is more than five decades old. In the computer programming world, that is ancient history.

A cryptocurrency removes the need for the middleman to transfer funds. It can be a store of value. It can be something that is easily sent and spent without needing a bank account. Transactions take place on a secure network. They can be fast, transparent and easier to establish audit trails. They may even shorten the time it takes to pay workers from every two weeks to immediately because the bookkeeping steps can be instantaneous. They can allow stock exchange transactions to settle immediately instead of T + 2 settlement, which is the trade date plus two days.

---

[8] Pantera Capital, *Blockchain Letter,* 8/4/21, https://panteracapital.com/blockchain-letter/esg-is-the-little-bighorn-of-bitcoin-skeptics/

49

When I learned about XRP, it was an obvious improvement over bitcoin and a technology that was badly needed to improve our banking system. I still don't like bitcoin because it seems like other cryptocurrencies have already surpassed its rudimentary technology. Bitcoin requires massive amounts of computers and energy to mine into existence; it takes more energy than the country of Argentina uses each year. It is also very slow, has high fees and is not sustainable. If enough of the population adopted bitcoin, it would use all the energy on the planet. Sorry, bitcoin lovers, but I just don't see how bitcoin is the long-term winner with all those negatives.

Once I started researching other cryptocurrencies, I realized that this new technology is part of the Quantum Age we are going into, and I learned assets will be digitized and tokenized into small slices of value that allow us to digitally divide anything into smaller pieces and give each piece value. I saw how we will invest in pieces of property like commercial buildings, farmland, bonds, rental units, businesses, racehorses, precious metals — anything of value. Each token is unique, recorded on the blockchain and unhackable.

The Concept of Money is Changing

I also realized that paper money was a very antiquated concept. It doesn't make sense to have to carry heavy bars of gold or silver around with you. That is sort of how paper money came into existence: exchanging a paper receipt for metals. In the 1860s, our federal government legal tender said "silver certificate" because it was redeemable for silver. But now paper currencies aren't backed by gold or silver anymore. They are fiat currencies and that means that they are backed by nothing of value and at risk of losing value (by inflation) if too much supply is created. Well, what are we seeing today? We are seeing central banks all over the world issue a lot more supply of currency than they used to and that means the currencies are at risk of devaluation. We will talk more about that later.

Some billionaires are worried about devaluation and are investing to compensate for it. John Malone is the former CEO of a huge cable and media giant, TCI, and the largest landowner in America. He is concerned about the devaluation of our currency, so he is spending (trading) fiat U.S. dollars for farmland in an attempt to maintain his money's purchasing power. Other billionaires such as Ted Turner, Jeff Bezos and Bill Gates have also bought land, ranches or farms. Physical assets are in limited supply and hold their value when the supply of fiat currencies is expanding exponentially.

Cryptocurrencies that are limited in the amount issued can solve the problem of currency devaluation. The one thing I liked about bitcoin was it had a limited amount created: 21 million. Only 13 million bitcoins are in circulation or stashed away in wallets. If you create a digital asset and guarantee that only a limited number will ever be created, I see how that can maintain its value and eliminate inflation. It will eliminate the problem of money printing or too much creation and devaluing its worth.

Soon Wall Street investors who are billionaires were talking about how they were buying bitcoin; people like Stanley Druckenmiller, Bill Miller and Paul Tudor Jones. That got my attention because I heard a lot of hedge funds wanted to invest in bitcoin and cryptocurrencies for their ultra-high-net-worth clients. They were attracted by the high compounding rates. It appears bitcoin was simply moving in a four-year cycle.

I was starting to see indications of some very wealthy people moving into cryptocurrencies and that really piqued my curiosity, but I was very uncomfortable with not knowing who founded bitcoin. I only want to own investments where I know who the creator is and the management team behind them. I'm a very conservative investor generally, and this was not something I could ignore. All of those things and a lot of skepticism initially went through my head when I researched cryptocurrency.

Some cryptocurrencies have impressive technology and ambitious plans. Others seem to be purely speculative. There are cryptocurrencies that will revamp the entire bill payment structure we currently have because in our currency financial system, the SWIFT banking system software (costly and slow), for example, doesn't talk to PayPal's software. In a global world, we need banking and payment software that works globally and outside the traditional banking system with new FinTech.

In my research, XRP made a lot of sense. To me, it seemed like the next version of bitcoin or bitcoin 2.0. It improved on some of the limitations of bitcoin, like consuming too much energy to mine it. It used a technology called "Proof of Stake" that reduced the energy usage substantially. Bitcoin's required amount of energy usage is not going to work for a mass-adopted cryptocurrency. Nor will having to wait 15 minutes or more for each transaction to go through.

First Mover Technology Doesn't Always Keep the Lead

Sometimes, first movers in the tech space can become obsolete and are not the big wealth generators they seem to promise, such as when search engines were introduced. Do you remember there was a company called Netscape that was the big first search engine? Netscape was introduced with fanfare. Then Google came along and basically the masses adopted it. Google became the standard and the winning stock, not Netscape.

That is how I see where we are with bitcoin. I think there is going to be a next-level bitcoin (XRP) that is going to improve upon it. That is where the mass adoption happens. But one of the reasons that bitcoin reached the incredible price of over $60,000 a coin is because it has clarity from the Securities and Exchange Commission (SEC) that it is "not a security." Bitcoin and Ethereum have that clarity, and other coins do not. Because those two coins have that special clarity from regulators, they have been able to gain in value.

Bitcoin Shares the Spotlight with Ethereum

The second cryptocurrency, Ethereum, was created in 2015. Ethereum is also a decentralized, open-source block chain, but it allows for smart contract functionality. Smart contracts allow you to automate certain legal or financial agreements through a transaction protocol that executes the agreement automatically. Ethereum is now the second-largest cryptocurrency by market capitalization.

Will bitcoin and Ethereum remain dominant, or will something else capture market share? An important point to understand about cryptocurrencies is what they will be used for, or the "use case." There are more than 11,000 cryptocurrencies as I write this. Only some have legitimate use cases; others are more akin to securities that you buy for capital appreciation. In my opinion, having a use case is critical for cryptocurrencies to have long-term success and growth.

From a regulatory perspective, how have bitcoin and Ethereum been the only two cryptocurrencies that have gotten clarity and the blessing of the SEC that they are not securities? I'm not exactly sure, but I do know that Senator Tom Cotton of Arkansas wrote a letter to the director of national intelligence, John Ratcliff, and national security advisor, Robert O'Brien. In his letter, he stated that he wants *"the SEC to develop a clearer articulation of policy and ultimately formal commission guidance, addressing digital currencies to ensure U.S. companies have the chance to lead."* And he goes on to say, *"So far, the commission has concluded that only two digital assets should be considered non-securities, Chinese controlled Bitcoin and Ether."*[9] Those are his direct words. He is asking for clarification on these digital assets so they are categorized as non-securities and can move forward, have legitimacy and compete with other Chinese digital assets because China is working on a digital yuan right now. We will eventually have regulatory clarity, in my opinion.

It is my contention that over time, XRP will be the best performer of them all and "the standard" for cross-border payments and central bank digital currencies. We will talk more about what gives cryptocurrency worth and why XRP is so special.

---

[9] Alisha Roy, *AMBCrypto,* 11/25/20, https://eng.ambcrypto.com/us-intelligence-chief-concerned-about-chinese-dominance-in-cryptocurrency/

Cryptocurrencies are Not Inflationary; They are Superior Money

What could really cause quicker adoption of cryptocurrency would be something like fiat currencies losing value. Understand that the U.S. dollar has already lost 96% of its value since 1913. What I mean is 96% of its purchasing power is gone by inflation. That is why we see real estate at such exorbitant prices right now; it is because the value of the dollar has declined. Our purchasing power has declined that much, and it looks like houses have gained in value by a lot, but it is really our purchasing power that has been lost.

What happens if our purchasing power loses even more? Many of our fruits and vegetables are imported, so a weak dollar means those are going to skyrocket in price. When you see the purchasing power of the dollar lose value, it is going to appear like massive inflation is occurring. With the balance sheet of the Federal Reserve expanding and then printing money like crazy, and the value of the dollar declining, people are going to wonder where else they can store their money — what can I put my money into other than cash that can be a store of value? For some, that might be bitcoin; for others, it might be gold or silver; and, for others, other cryptocurrencies are interesting. Just know that any issue in the banking sector or with a weakening dollar might cause the fleeing of money into cryptocurrencies and digital assets.

Cryptocurrencies can be deflationary if they limit the quantity in existence and/or they decrease in total supply each time they are used. When a cryptocurrency is sent to someone, a tiny amount is burned, thereby decreasing the supply. This is how they will retain their value and not have the problems of fiat currencies that can be created without limits.

Ripple Labs, Inc., an American company for global payments and liquidity, has a cryptocurrency, XRP, to be used as a bridge between any currencies or tokenized value to exchange from one to another quickly, efficiently and at a very low cost. The time to transfer funds between banks is cut from days to about 3 seconds, costing a fraction of a penny per transaction.

Yes, XRP caught my attention because it was the solution for fast cross-border payments, was energy-efficient, low-cost and a bridge asset to any other currency. Each time it is used, one drop or $.000001 is used to send it. This particular cryptocurrency is up already 357% in the last year, outperforming bitcoin, and I don't think that we are anywhere close to being done with this. I think we are just at the very beginning of this journey and for a lot of reasons, such as this cryptocurrency must go a lot higher to make it easier and less costly to use as a payment system or as a store of value.

Humanity is Being Freed from Centralized Control of Money

We are moving from a centralized banking system to a decentralized financial system (known as "DeFi"), meaning no longer will a small group of people at central banks control the money supply. The nature of money is changing, and the way we are going to earn and grow money is changing. Thank goodness! We have been in a centralized-control monopoly system that has to be modernized. In the future, banks won't be needed for loans or savings accounts. They may manage money, it may be robo-advised or we may do it ourselves, but every aspect of financial services is on the table right now for massive change -- in a good way.

Since the U.S. dollar is no longer backed by gold, it is easy for the Federal Reserve to create unlimited amounts of it and cause its purchasing power to decline. However, with cryptocurrencies, a limited number is created so they remain scarce and valuable. They are decentralized, meaning there is no central bank or centralized organization that is in control, and they are permissionless, meaning you don't need anyone's permission to transfer them. Not a bank, not Western Union, not the government, not the Fed.

Now I want to share with you why cryptocurrency is a great new technology, possibly the most lucrative investment opportunity I have seen yet, and why it deserves your attention and perhaps to be an investment in a portion of your portfolio.

Cryptocurrencies are a Big Improvement Over Centralized, Debt-Based Currency

Besides being a great technology for wealth-building, crypto-currencies also solve a very big problem in the world: centralized control of currencies and devaluation of the dollar. The money system we currently have is a centralized system, controlled by the Federal Reserve. In 1918, the Federal Reserve was voted in by Congress as the central bank of the United States and our currency became the Federal Reserve Note. A note is debt. Every dollar that comes into existence is borrowed and adds to the U.S. debt. This became problematic for foreign countries in 1971, when the U.S. was spending a lot of money on the Vietnam War and international aid. The agreement of 44 countries after WWII at Bretton Woods, New Hampshire, in 1944, was that they would fix their currencies to the dollar and the dollar would be fixed to gold.

In the 1960s, European and Japanese exports became more competitive with U.S. exports. The U.S. share of world output decreased and so did the need for dollars, making converting those dollars to gold more desirable. The deteriorating U.S. balance of payments, combined with military spending and foreign aid, resulted in a large supply of dollars around the world. Meanwhile, the gold supply had increased only marginally. Eventually, there were more foreign-held dollars than the United States had gold. The country was vulnerable to a run on gold and there was a loss of confidence in the U.S. government's ability to meet its obligations, thereby threatening both the dollar's position as reserve currency and the overall Bretton Woods system.[10]

Foreign countries started requesting to be paid in gold. On August 15, 1971, President Nixon removed us from the gold standard to stop international convertibility from the dollar to gold and the U.S. gold supply from draining away. Ever since, there has been nothing of value backing the U.S. dollar. That is

---

[10] FederalReserveHistory.org, https://www.federalreservehistory.org/essays/gold-convertibility-ends

what is called a "fiat" currency. Its only backing is the full faith and credit of the U.S. government and the military.

Since the Federal Reserve controls the money supply and they are continuously creating more, we have inflation, which erodes our purchasing power. More than 40% of all the dollars that exist today have been printed in the last 18 months. That means our currency is being devalued at an even greater rate. Currently, the U.S. debt is $29 trillion, most of which is interest on the debt, but that amount does not include unfunded liabilities such as Social Security, Medicare, Medicaid and other benefits that have been promised but not reserved for. Taking these programs into account, the estimated debt in the U.S. is over $133 trillion. Foreign countries have record levels of debt, too. The world has never been drowning in debt as much as it is today.

The Federal Reserve's mandate is to provide maximum employment, stable prices and moderate inflation, but we are far from that at the moment. Currently, inflation is running higher than it has for years, but that is not completely accurate because of the way the government changed the way it calculates inflation. The newer method gives the impression that inflation has been running at a lower rate than it actually has.

According to John Williams at ShadowStats.com, if the inflation calculation that was used in the 1970s were still used today, the inflation rate would be about 7% higher than what is being reported to us. We all notice that prices in groceries, home values, rent and energy are much higher than when we were younger. The real rate of inflation is far beyond the 2% annual rate reported to us. This has the effect of keeping our wages and pensions lower, reducing our spending power, and penalizing savings accounts with low interest rates. In effect, it is making the rich, who can afford to buy assets that increase with inflation, richer and the poor poorer.

As I said before, the greater the supply of currency in existence, the less it is worth. What will help in the future is to have a cryptocurrency that is decentralized where the amount is limited. Central banks won't be able to create any more cryptocurrency because they are not in control of it. It is decentralized and no one is in control. Transactions rely on a consensus protocol. Ripple doesn't use blockchain but uses a distributed consensus ledger with a network of authenticating servers and crypto tokens (XRP). Fees for processing transactions are much lower than bitcoin. Cryptocurrency can also help countries that have an unstable currency and open up the network of individuals and industries they can work with.

Central banks are going to create a digital version of their currencies. There will be a digital yuan, a digital euro, a digital ruble, etc. The first central bank digital currency (CBDC) was issued by the Bahamas and is appropriately called the Sand Dollar. I believe eventually all currencies worldwide will be available in a digital format.

Bitcoin is not the crypto that will be used as currency. It is best used as a store of value. As previously mentioned, it does not have smart contracts, uses too much energy, and is too costly and slow. Christine Lagarde, president of the European Central Bank, has already said bitcoin will never be used as a currency. However, XRP can act as a bridge to other currencies. It can move across borders quickly and inexpensively. It is decentralized and is perfect for smart contracts. It could even be backed by assets someday, which would make it preferable to fiat currency.

In the next chapter, I will share what makes cryptocurrencies valuable and later I will tell you how you can select the dominant winners to invest in. I think XRP is the one cryptocurrency that is going to dominate this decade and for a lot of years to come.

The Bottom Line

Cryptocurrencies are not just about investment. They will change almost everything we do financially on a big scale and in everyday living. Understanding this change will make you look at the world in a whole new way.

Leap into the Quantum Age

Cryptocurrencies are slowly becoming integrated into our financial system. Where have you noticed cryptocurrencies in your daily life? Have you seen them offered by PayPal or Venmo? At a bank ATM? Accepted by a gas station, sporting event (Dallas Mavericks) or convenience store?

Chapter 6
Cryptocurrencies to Invest In

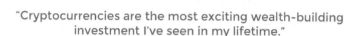

"Cryptocurrencies are the most exciting wealth-building investment I've seen in my lifetime."

Now you know something about cryptocurrencies such as bitcoin, Ethereum and XRP. You know about the high compounding rates and that assets can be digitized and tokenized — but there is so much more. Since we are still early in this technology, it is still progressing. Each record or blockchain has to talk to each other, work with one another and be "interoperable."

The ISO 20022 Standard

One way banks are getting more standardized is by adopting regulations that allow them to talk to each other by using the same digital formatting. That way, a computer in Singapore can understand the banking instructions from a computer in the United Arab Emirates. These protocols, called ISO 20022 (ISO = International Standards Organization), are set to take effect in November of 2021. The ISO 20022 standard will change the way banks relay cross-border payments instructions. While ISO 20022 is not mandatory from a regulatory perspective, *those that don't comply now risk being excluded from international payment systems.*

The cryptocurrencies that we will examine are on blockchains that may be built for different purposes. Sometimes, one has an advantage over another. Out of thousands of cryptocurrencies, perhaps 100 will survive because they have real use cases. Knowing this gives us an edge over many people who haven't studied this. They likely will be shocked when their cryptocurrency cannot meet requirements for regulations.

The cryptocurrencies that we know are ISO 20022-compliant so far are XRP, XLM, XDC, IOTA, ALGO and stable coin USDC. Dogecoin, Litecoin and Flare Sparks have use cases with smart contracts. This is like being able to stake crypto or put it on deposit and earn high interest rates. By being your own bank, you can earn passive income.

Please remember that I am writing this book early in a technological revolution and in a volatile world, where many things are changing. This is only the beginning. However, we know the ISO 20022-compliant cryptocurrencies are the ones that have already been selected by financial institutions that have to plan years in advance. By 2022, it is estimated that over 80% of high-value transactions will be done using ISO 20022.

What Makes Cryptocurrency Valuable?

Some people are confused by what makes cryptocurrency valuable. Seven main factors give cryptocurrency value.

1. *The "use case" or what does it do?* The use case means it has to have some ability to accomplish something, and not just be a "store of value." Bitcoin was the first iteration of cryptocurrency, and it was simply "a store of value," kind of like digital gold. You put money into it and the value can grow or decline. Bitcoin uses up some of its supply every time there is a transaction, so it is becoming scarcer. That tends to help its value climb over time. Cryptocurrencies that came after bitcoin started to have functionality.

   Ethereum, the second-largest cryptocurrency, is an open-source technology, which allows developers to build on the technology and create other cryptocurrencies from it. That is why some developers who create new cryptocurrencies give 50% of the supply to Vitalik Buterin, the Russian-Canadian founder of Ethereum (with other developers).

   Buterin compared bitcoin to a pocket calculator that can do one thing well, and Ethereum to a smart phone with multiple applications you can use. Ethereum hosts smart contracts — collections of code that carry out instructions and run on the blockchain. They are like apps on a smartphone and aren't controlled by anybody. A big trend in Ethereum is decentralized finance (DeFi), where traditional financial products like mortgages and loans are created using the blockchain. Like Flare Sparks, which are bringing smart contract functionality to XRP but on a separate blockchain, this will essentially allow you to deposit your cryptocurrency and earn interest, like being your own bank.

2. *How much money does it handle?* The amount of money that runs on the cryptocurrency, either by investing in it to hold it or using it for transactions, will affect its value. As you will see, XRP was created to handle central bank digital currencies or CBDCs. By being the bridge asset, it can easily convert one currency into another. Central banks move trillions of dollars around the world. If we add the value of derivatives, you could make the case that central banks will run quadrillions of dollars over the rails of the XRP ledger, making it the most valuable cryptocurrency of all.

3. *How many coins are there?* Scarcity brings value in anything, so the fewer coins that are available and if they are limited, theoretically, the higher their value. However, that is not the only consideration and must be taken into account with the other factors.

4. *What is the adoption rate?* The faster a cryptocurrency is adopted, the faster the price rises. If several companies start accepting your cryptocurrency as money, or more developers start using your blockchain to enable faster, greener transactions, that is a huge boost since it will be adopted by more people faster.

5. *How in demand is it?* An increase in demand will increase the price.

6. *Has it received favorable press?* Positive press can affect a cryptocurrency's rate of adoption and success.

7. *How large is the community?* How many people are invested in it? How many companies support the use of the cryptocurrency? How broadly owned is it worldwide? For example, Dogecoin is a global sensation with investors and is already accepted as currency by 38 companies. We fully expect Amazon, Facebook, Nike and Tesla may accept it soon.

All of these factors make a difference when valuing cryptocurrencies. The reason XRP is my #1 pick is you can see how it checks all of the boxes and because it will be the banking standard for central bank digital currencies; and its ledger rails will run the most assets in the world.

XRP

XRP really impressed me when I saw its potential to modernize the antiquated banking system worldwide. Currently, to send money across the world today, it is faster to put money in a suitcase and get on a plane than to send it through the SWIFT system. In the age of modern computers, that is a sad truth.

The SWIFT system was created in 1973. This antiquated technology is really a messaging system and suffers from high fees and a process so slow the money can take several days to transfer — especially if you have to convert it into another currency. For foreign currency, conversion banks keep *$27 trillion sitting idle* in what are called Nostro Vostro accounts — Latin words meaning "ours" and "yours." The terms are used when one bank has another bank's money on deposit (typically in relation to international trading or other financial transactions) in case someone needs to convert from one currency to another. Can you imagine $27 trillion dollars permanently on hold in case it is needed to convert currency? That is an incredibly inefficient use of funds. The banking system needs a way to transfer money fast with low fees and very high accuracy and reliability. That is exactly the problem that XRP solves.

Moving quickly through the banking industry, XRP has already been adopted by more than 300 financial institutions. When Bank of America adopted XRP, they saw an increased investment from Warren Buffet and that was after he sold off most of his other bank holdings. He has also invested in SBI Holdings of Japan, which is one of the original venture capital investors in Ripple. It is said they own 10% of Ripple.

In 2004, software developer Ryan Fugger conceived the idea for RipplePay. The company was sold to Jed McCaleb, Arthur Britto and David Schwartz, who wanted to use it for their future digital currency network. In 2011, they created the XRP Ledger and the new company was named OpenCoin. In 2013, they closed two angel rounds of funding and renamed OpenCoin as Ripple Labs. McCaleb left and started Mt. Gox, the bitcoin exchange, and a fork of Ripple called Stellar Lumens (XLM).

Ripple set out to improve on bitcoin's limitations (requires massive energy to mine, has high fees and is slow) and "create a digital asset that was more sustainable and built specifically for payments."[11]

This is a peer-to-peer network that can exist outside banks. With a total of $100 billion hard-coded into the software, the amount of money is finite. The only way that can change is by the complete network of XRP validators; however, Ripple only ever runs about 6%. In other words, there is no centralized control of XRP. Neither the central banks nor Ripple can control it. That is very good news because it means investors are not under the central control of any entity with power over our money and ultimately, the people.

Another benefit of XRP versus other blockchains is that the minimum fee per transaction, which is .00001 XRP, is burned. This, coupled with the finite amount of XRP existing, makes XRP a deflationary currency (not inflationary like fiat currencies).

---

[11] XRPL.org website, Provide a Better Alternative to Bitcoin, https://xrpl.org/history.html

XRP Will Make Sending Currency as Easy as Sending Email

I believe XRP has the potential to be the Internet of Value. It can digitally bridge old currencies such as the fiat U.S. dollar with new currencies such as asset-backed currencies, thus creating digital commodities, stocks, insurance, loans and more. It will allow you to exchange anything into anything, from one digitized store of value to another, quickly and with minimal cost, as easily as sending an email message. Working with central banks, money changers and other financial institutions, it will change the banking industry and how money is exchanged and transferred forever.

Once again, I will mention the weaknesses of bitcoin: It uses massive energy, is slow to process and has high fees. That is the exact opposite of what you would want to use as a currency. Although bitcoin was the first cryptocurrency, Ripple CEO, Brad Garlinghouse, likens what he thinks will happen with bitcoin to what happened with Napster, the first digital music file-sharing company:

> *"Comparing bitcoin to Napster as an early player that demonstrated the digital aspect of music and proved the technology but didn't win, Garlinghouse said bitcoin may prove to be a better store of value than a medium for transaction — its average transaction time is over 10 hours at a cost of more than $1, he said, while Ripple can process a transaction in three to four seconds for a fraction of a penny."[12]*

Napster, of course, was the streaming music company that enabled people to distribute music across the Internet for free. It was a first-mover technology, only to be replaced by the iPod, which became the standard. In the same way, I agree with Garlinghouse and believe XRP is superior to bitcoin for global payments and foreign currency exchange.

---

[12] Tom Groenfeldt, *Forbes.com,* 8/16/17,
https://www.forbes.com/sites/tomgroenfeldt/2017/08/16/ripple-uses-blockchain-to-move-money-faster-than-a-flying-courier/?sh=3f9c5e8f3f3a.

As David Schwartz, Chief Technology Officer of Ripple, said, *"If XRP isn't the best, it doesn't deserve to succeed. We're not trying to fight for a bigger slice of a tiny pie but for the biggest slice we can get of all the payments in the world."[13]* He has made a case for XRP's price to reach $120 or more. I think that is a very conservative number. As Garlinghouse says, *"We are going to drive a massive demand for XRP because we are solving a multi-trillion dollar problem."[14]*

Why is XRP's Price Still Low?

One of the things that has held XRP's price down is lack of regulatory clarity. Years ago, bitcoin was given clarity that it wasn't a security by the Securities and Exchange Commission (SEC). That allowed investors to buy it and its price to increase. Unfortunately, in December of 2020, SEC Chair Jay Clayton brought a lawsuit against Ripple, claiming it *was* a security. The next day, he quit the SEC. The circumstances in which he brought the case are suspicious, and a lawsuit is ongoing.

While the regulators have not yet said that XRP is not a security, it is rumored that regulatory clarity is coming soon. Some people like me believe that regulatory clarity will send XRP much higher. What we are looking for is referred to as a level playing field. When U.S. regulators provide clarity that XRP is not a security, it will give legitimacy for XRP to be invested in by large institutions and investment firms.

One thing we know for sure: *Every single country outside the U.S. that uses XRP has already determined it is a currency, not a security.* I am highly confident Ripple will win the lawsuit and prove it is not a security. Many exchanges have delisted XRP and will not allow you to buy it while the lawsuit is ongoing, which has severely hampered its price appreciation. Nonetheless, the performance of XRP has been astounding, actually outperforming bitcoin from April 2020 through April 2021,

[13] David Schwartz, *Twitter.com*, 11/25/18,
https://twitter.com/stedas/status/1066832740979494914?lang=en
[14] Brad Garlinghouse, *Twitter.com*, 4/30/19,
https://twitter.com/mark_phillips/status/1123198756265000960?lang=en

despite the lawsuit. The good news is the lawsuit has held XRP's price low, so you can still buy it for around $1.00.

There are many positive events yet to happen for XRP and Ripple that we can look forward to: the end of the Ripple lawsuit; exchanges re-listing XRP; Ripple going public in a U.S. initial public offering (IPO); Ripple IPO going live on stock exchanges and becoming known by more people; Ripple becoming the standard for international money transfers between banks; and finally, blockchains and distributed ledger solutions maturing, and all asset exchange networks becoming interoperable.

Brian Brooks, former director of the Office of Comptroller of the Currency (OCC), says clarity of regulations is needed: *"But with more clarity, institutions that see this more as a real thing are going to adopt at scale which they already started to do."*[15] The regulations are what will bring the big investor money into XRP.

XRP has already been following the laws for anti-money laundering and anti-terrorism, so it is ready to go. We are very close to this happening. As soon as the regulations are released, the big money in the U.S. is going to come in, in my opinion. XRP is solving the largest financial problem on the planet. It is dealing with global governments — 95% of XRP customers are outside the U.S. That means XRP will not have billions or trillions, but a quadrillion dollars or more running on the rails of the XRP ledger. It is so enormous that it is the global dominating winner. This is not a stock; think of it more like a global currency.

Where will XRP's price eventually go? Well, let's do a simple back-of-the-envelope calculation. A conservative estimate of all financial instruments (stocks, bonds, currencies, real estate, derivatives, etc.) is $1.4 quadrillion. If XRP were to be used as the Internet of Value for just 10% of this market valuation, XRP is worth $1,009.81 per coin. In my opinion, its final destination is much higher than that. I am so confident in

---

[15] Danny Nelson, *Coindesk.com,* 12/4/20, https://www.coindesk.com/policy/2020/12/04/occ-chief-hints-at-coming-good-actions-on-crypto-by-end-of-trumps-term/

XRP's future, I believe if you were to buy only one cryptocurrency, this is "the one" to own.

In summary, why is XRP already in the lead? While we don't know all of the plans central banks have, what we do know is:

- XRP already has 300 financial institutions as clients; is on 200 exchanges and at 3,000 ATMs; partners with MoneyGram, Apple and Amazon; and is so far ahead, it is tracking to be the standard for central bank digital currencies.

- It has 90% of its clients outside the U.S., many of which are governments, that have already declared XRP a currency, not a security.

- XRP has handled more than $1 trillion in total transactions.

- Flare Sparks enable the ability for smart contracts (some say this may allow XRP to overtake the #2 largest crypto by market capitalization, Ethereum).

- The SEC case is against Ripple. XRP was already declared a currency, not a security, by U.S. governmental agencies in 2015. If Ripple went away, XRP would still survive. Ripple's lawyers have said: *"Other major branches of the U.S. government, including the Justice Department and the Treasury Department's FinCen, have already determined that XRP is a currency. Transactions in XRP thus fall outside the scope of the federal securities laws."*[16]

- Game over and regulatory clarity incoming. Boom!

Flare Sparks and XRP

The Flare Network is a group of talented computer developers who have decided to bring smart contract capability

---

[16] Kevin Shalvey, *Markets.BusinessInsider.com,* 12/23/20, https://markets.businessinsider.com/news/currencies/sec-says-ripples-xrp-crypto-is-13-billion-unregistered-offering-2020-12

to the XRP ecosystem. Flare Sparks are a standalone crypto with the symbol FLR and can be held or sold on exchanges. It will trade on crypto exchanges with its own value. Owners of XRP on December 12, 2020, were expected to receive free Sparks from Flare Networks in September 2021 on approximately a 1:1.0073 basis. Flare Sparks will enable smart contracts to be added to the XRP ledger.

Smart contracts are a computer protocol that automatically executes terms of a contract or agreement. Think about the process after you have an accepted offer on a house. Next comes the escrow, title search, loans, legal documents, etc. All of that process can be automated with smart contracts. You have conditions to perform and either you perform or you don't. Smart contracts can handle it all automatically.

The exciting thing about smart contract technology is it means you can receive passive income and be your own bank. Besides free FLR tokens, there is a second free airdrop of DFLR tokens. DFLR can be converted into YFLR, which will give you five opportunities to earn passive income by loaning your XRP for yield on mutual funds, insurance, loans, etc. The five categories are Flare Loan, FlareX, Flare Farm, Flare Wrap and Flare Mutual. I won't go into detail explaining them, but just know they are various forms of providing passive income to you.

You don't need to invest in FLR to earn interest, you can "mint" your coins by depositing XRP. The definition of minting is the computer process of validating information by creating a new block and recording that information into the blockchain. The blockchain is simply like a book of records. New pages are created to store more information, which are pages in the blockchain. That means you deposit a required amount of crypto and earn interest on it.

Flare recently announced a few more airdrops. Songbird (SGB) will be given in the ratio of 1 XRP to 0.1511 and only to holders of XRP who owned it on December 12, 2020. Flare CEO Hugo Philion, says, "It is for testing of the integrity if the proposed production network (Flare), proposed governance updates over time, the Flare core protocols and dApps launching on Flare."[17]

Two other free airdrops will be given to XRP holders, regardless of when they purchased it. First, Evernote (EVRS), is a "layer two-node ecosystem that is looking to deploy on the XRP ledger." Second, Aesthetes is dropping its native token (ELS). This is an NFT art project that will launch on the XRP ledger. Flare Sparks (FLR) and now EVRS and ELS will be cryptocurrencies that will have their own value and trade independently, so participating in an airdrop like this is like receiving free money; kind of like when you get a dividend on a stock. Everyone who owns XRP will get the same amount of EVRS and ELS.

Stellar Lumens (XLM)

Another ISO 20022 cryptocurrency we are investing in is Stellar Lumens (trading symbol XLM). It was created by Jed McCaleb, co-founder of Ripple Labs. He created a cross-border payment system that acts like a bridge between digital currencies and fiat currencies. Like XRP, it is a low-cost, open-source, decentralized protocol for transferring fiat currency to digital currency quickly. It allows cross-border transactions between any pair of currencies. This is widely believed to be for the "unbanked" population and for anyone with a phone to use as a currency exchange and/or payment method. (Unbanked simply means you don't have a bank account.)

In the U.S., it is estimated that 6% to 7% of Americans do not have a bank account. This could be because they lack identification, have a poor or no credit history, and can't meet the minimum balance requirement. There are 1.7 billion people globally who do not have a bank account.[18] That is almost a quarter of the world's population.

---

[17] *Techtelegraph.co.uk website,* 7/22/21, https://techtelegraph.co.uk/airdrop-incoming-xrp-holders-to-get-free-tokens-for-flares-new-canary-network/

[18] The Unbanked, World Bank, 2017, https://globalfindex.worldbank.org/sites/globalfindex/files/chapters/2017%20Findex%20full%20report_chapter2.pdf

XLM is the perfect solution for people without a bank. They can send and receive money through an app on their phone. It is nearly instantaneous and costs next to nothing to send. XRP is for cross-border payments and CBDCs, while XLM is for everyday people. They are complementary technologies that are considered "brother and sister" to each other.

I believe both will be very successful and financially lucrative investments. XLM is my #2 choice for investing, after XRP. XRP should be your largest holding by far.

Dogecoin

Of all of our cryptocurrencies, the most colorful and fun is the one known as Dogecoin or Doge. It has been around since 2013, but it is new to a lot of people because of the attention it has been getting. It has also been getting big returns and acceptance.

What is it? Dogecoin is a cryptocurrency that is a peer-to-peer form of money. Like our other cryptocurrencies, it means there is no central bank in the middle organizing it. A decentralized form of currency, it was said to have started as a joke. It was a fork (a variation) off the blockchain of another cryptocurrency called Litecoin. Litecoin was created from a fork of the bitcoin core blockchain to reduce transaction fees.

I recommended investing in Dogecoin, because it gained legitimacy when the Flare Network said they were going to build on the Doge platform. That meant adding a functionality to Doge that would make it a smart contract and allow you to essentially be your own bank and collect multiple forms of passive income. When it became legitimized by the Flare Network, it had to be added to our recommended list of cryptocurrencies.

Doge may become the "people's currency," which is its nickname. I think what we are seeing is people choosing what cryptocurrency they want to use. It is not just here in the United States; it is all around the world. One morning, I woke up to a 35% increase in the price of Dogecoin. The Asian markets were buying Dogecoin while I slept. This is a worldwide phenomenon.

Thirty-eight companies have already approved the use of Dogecoin as a currency to buy their products. Mark Cuban, billionaire owner of the Dallas Mavericks basketball team, says his company will accept Dogecoin for payment of Mavericks tickets and merchandise. Amazon, PayPal, eBay, AMC Theaters and all kinds of payment companies and other retailers are looking into possibly accepting Dogecoin. This could be the first widely accepted cryptocurrency for the consumer. Another reason that Dogecoin's value has been skyrocketing is that it has been added to new cryptocurrency exchanges so you can buy it in more places now.

How did Doge start? It was created on December 6, 2013, by a pair of software engineers. As a joke, Billy Marcus, an IBM programmer from Portland, Oregon, set out to differentiate his crypto from bitcoin, which was steeped in mystery with an anonymous creator. He attracted a small niche group of miners. Marcus wanted his cryptocurrency to be open to the masses. He looked for help in making his dream a reality and found it in Jackson Palmer, who worked for Adobe. Palmer purchased the domain Dogecoin, a nod to the Doge meme with the Shiba Inu mascot that was all over the Internet at the time. Dogecoin is no longer a joke. Its popularity has soared astronomically, buoyed in part by its wide, mainstream adoption and love worldwide.

Elon Musk has been the loudest and most prominent supporter of Dogecoin. One bizarre tweet to his 50 million followers sent the crypto surging. That happened in April 2021 when Musk tweeted "doge barking at the moon" and shared an image of the painting by Spanish artist Juan Miro titled "Dog barking at the moon." The next month, in an appearance on Saturday Night Live, he proclaimed himself "the Dogefather."

Dogecoin has also enjoyed something of a cult status on the Internet message board Reddit. A popular group there decided to buy it, propelling its value over 600%. Dogecoin currently has a staggering 129.5 billion coins in circulation.

Remember: Traditional currencies trade trillions of dollars every single day. The markets for currencies are much bigger than for securities, so people don't understand how the numbers can get so big. That is because they are comparing them to stocks and not to currencies. The returns have been astounding and are also much greater than securities. A $1,000 investment in Doge on January 1, 2021 was worth $115,000 in May 2021.

With Doge gaining more accessibility and being accepted by more stores and establishments, I think its value is only going to grow. Cuban has said he will never sell even one Dogecoin and even has his 11-year-old son buying them. If Doge is accepted by Amazon as a form of payment, people have speculated it could spike Dogecoin's price by 10 times, so there is still room for future appreciation.

Doge has been doing fantastic, but we are probably starting another bull market. The cryptocurrency trend that peaked in 2017 left us chart patterns and certain statistics that we can refer back to and compare to today. It is almost the mirror image of the early stages of that 2017 bull market. When it started to take off during that time, bitcoin was losing some of its dominance. That means that money was flowing out of bitcoin and into some of the small cryptocurrencies, also called "alt coins."

Cryptocurrencies such as Dogecoin started to do well, and Dogecoin kicked off that bull market back in 2017, so it could be that Dogecoin is kicking off the next alt coin bull market. It is happening all over again, only this time, the dominance that bitcoin has been losing wasn't just over a few months. It has been happening for longer than a year, which might be telling us that the bull market that results from this will continue longer than the last one in 2017. I think we are going to see bitcoin lose more dominance, from being 50% of the $2 trillion market value of the cryptocurrency market like it is today.

Where does Dogecoin go from here? Well, today it is the fourth-largest cryptocurrency behind bitcoin, Ethereum and Binance coin. And that is saying a lot. I think we are seeing people adopt a peer-to-peer currency. They are choosing the one they want to use as a spendable digital form of money, and we are going to see more widespread adoption and announcements from companies that they are going to accept Dogecoin as payment. The more "use" it has, the more valuable it can be. We will see if more companies start to announce that they are accepting Doge as a form of payment. That is good news — that increases its usability, and that will increase its value. This is where we are going. It is the next version of the Internet, and it is going to be incredibly valuable.

As I said, Dogecoin is up 8,696% in a year. A $1,000 investment in Dogecoin became $86,960. Is that a bad thing? Is it bad because it grew fast? Why would it be bad to have 3% to 5% of your portfolio in a fast-growing asset? I can't answer that because there is no logic to it. The answer is always, "The tortoise wins." But that is a story, not real life. Most people would agree that getting to a destination faster is usually better. Taking an airplane across the country is faster than driving. Driving to a destination is faster than walking. Why we are using the tortoise-and-hare story to praise slowness in investing makes zero sense to me. Compounding at a higher rate is faster and better. We will talk more about this myth later.

The reason I became interested in and took Dogecoin seriously is because of Flare Networks. Flare Networks created Flare Sparks, which I mentioned is the technology that will allow certain cryptos to become smart contracts. In other words, if Flare decided to associate their "Sparks" with your coin, it could make it much more functional and valuable. For example, XRP was the first token they said they would give a free airdrop of Sparks to. This would enable XRP to create six ways to create passive income. They would be able to act as a bank and make loans for mortgages or other needs. They would be able to act as an insurance company and accept premiums for risks (and diversify it among a large group so no one person had a lot of risk of loss if there was a loss). The point is that Sparks added the ability to create "smart contracts" in conjunction with certain tokens. One of the tokens they named after XRP was Dogecoin.

Algorand

Another of my favorite cryptocurrency investments is Algorand (trading symbol ALGO). Algorand is a DeFi cryptocurrency and blockchain technology that enables the simple creation of next-generation financial products like cryptocurrencies, stable coins, NFTs and real estate. It is a blockchain that is scalable and used for fast and secure transactions. It was developed by Silvio Micali, a Massachusetts Institute of Technology (MIT) professor, who has won awards in computer science.

Algorand and Simetria launched the first digital securities exchange in Israel. It pledges to be the greenest blockchain, with a carbon-negative network now and in the future. It is interoperable with other tokens on the XRP ledger and is compliant with ISO 20022 regulations. It will also be working with NFTs. ALGO is available for purchase on Coinbase and currently pays a 4% APY.

Litecoin

As I mentioned, Dogecoin is a fork from Litecoin. Litecoin was created in 2011 by Charles Lee, a former Google employee. It is a peer-to-peer cryptocurrency that aims to enable instant, near-zero cost payments between people or institutions. It was an early bitcoin spinoff, a "lite" version of bitcoin (trading symbol LTC) and is very similar to it. It can produce more coins than bitcoin, and its transaction speed is much faster, but those don't affect its usability or value. It was created as a peer-to-peer currency for payments, to transact without a bank or third-party intermediary.

So far, it has survived in a highly competitive space, with Flare Networks naming Litecoin as one of the cryptocurrencies that Flare Networks will integrate with to bring DeFi services to the currency, allowing LTC "to be used trustlessly on Flare with Ethereum-style smart contracts" and promising "interoperability and composability." Flare also plans to airdrop free Sparks (FLR) to holders of Litecoin in the fall of 2021.

XinFin Network

The XinFin Network is a blockchain for the financial part of the Internet of value, with global finance and trade companies involved. Founded by Atul Khekade, Ritesh Kakkad and Karan Bhardwaj, it had an Initial Coin Offering (ICO; the crypto version of an IPO), in 2018 and went live in 2019. It is designed to complement the legacy financial ecosystem by providing a permissioned blockchain that governments, enterprises and private firms can use.

Currently working with the Cord-a Network on trade finance and other enterprise use cases, it handles 2,000 trades per second and settles in 2 seconds for a cost of less than a penny. The trading symbol of its fuel token is XDC and it is ISO 20022-compliant.

IOTA

IOTA is the first distributed ledger built for the "Internet of Everything" — a network for exchanging value and data between humans and machines. IOTA protects the integrity and verifiability of data. It enables secure exchange of both value and data exponentially faster without any transaction fees. It will record and execute transactions between machines and devices in the Internet of Things (IoT) ecosystem. ISO 20022-compliant, it helps to enable a machine economy and is one of the most important and unique cryptocurrencies.

An Important Perspective on the Beginning of the Bubble

I would like to conclude this chapter to address any naysayers. A lot of financial publications and media are talking about this being the end of a crypto bubble, but I beg to differ. I have been through several bubbles in my lifetime, and I have gotten pretty good at identifying them. This is not the end of a bubble. It is the early innings of a technological revolution.

There is still a lot of criticism, negativity, fear, uncertainty and doubt about cryptocurrencies. That is not what happens at the peak of a bubble. An even better indicator of the peak is that Wall Street will have already sold it to millions of investors. This is far from the case. Cryptocurrency is still very misunderstood and even hated. When an asset is hated, that is the most bullish thing. When people can't stand it, when they think it is a joke, when they think it is terrible, that it can't ever succeed — those are all the things I love to hear because that is the exact opposite of bubble talk. We are so early in this trend that people don't understand how big this technological boom is or how much wealth it will create.

As I said earlier, it is much bigger than the Internet boom we went through over 20 years ago. By the end of the Internet boom, everybody — including the magazine covers — was proclaiming that it was going to continue forever. That was the peak of the bubble. We are years before the bubble, but it will come. We will talk more about how to identify bubbles in a later chapter.

Twenty years ago, the very first Internet companies were just being created. People really didn't understand what the Internet was, how it was going to change our lives and how ubiquitous it was about to become. Only technology companies had websites; now everyone has them. In 2008, only technology companies had apps; now many companies have them. Soon, using the blockchain and smart contracts will be a normal part of business.

That is what is happening with cryptocurrencies and blockchain technology, only this is much bigger than the Internet because the Internet was about communications, email, social media and basic commerce. The Quantum Age in regards to decentralized finance (DeFi) is about smart contracts on blockchains, without the need for brokerages, exchanges, or banks. It is the new Internet of Value redefining investing, tokenization, smart contracts, banking and currencies (money).

Just to review, all value is about to be tokenized, all things are going to be digitized and the blockchain is going to authenticate everything. It will get rid of all the fraud, duplication, fakes and forgeries. Tokenization is transforming how people buy, sell, track and manage assets — everything from art and real estate to intellectual property, equities, and supply chain goods. In fact, *the World Economic Forum projects 10% of the world's GDP will be tokenized by 2027.*

What is happening is so life-changing, and yet people have been discouraged and told to stay away from it. However, institutional investors are now raising a billion dollars to invest in cryptocurrencies. Top investing institutions like Harvard, Yale and Brown are quietly investing in cryptocurrencies. Affluent family offices — the wealthiest people in the country — are just starting to invest in cryptocurrencies, but the media is telling everyday investors not to buy them and that it is a bubble. A joke. That it is not going to last: "Don't bother investing in it. It is a bubble and too late."

Hogwash. This is the biggest investment opportunity for wealth creation we have seen in our lifetimes.

I have never seen a bigger investment opportunity than right now, although I have to warn you that cryptocurrencies are very volatile — they can be up 30% to 100% and down 30% to 50%. Sometimes that can happen in a day. They swing like crazy. But if you have a long-term outlook, like two to five years, and can put 3% to 5% of your portfolio into cryptocurrency, I think there are fabulous gains to be made.

You don't have to invest a lot of money. You can put a couple of hundred dollars in it, which is how I had my *Be Wealthy & Smart VIP* members start until they became more comfortable investing in cryptos. Initially, I recommended to invest a small amount until they got the hang of it, saw what the returns were and what an incredible investment opportunity it was. They enjoyed the returns and realized it was also fun to invest in. Once you learn the technology and how to use exchanges and wallets, it gets easier.

The Bottom Line

This early on in the phase of cryptocurrency investing, I wouldn't recommend selling any cryptocurrencies. Although the gains are mind-boggling and astounding, leading people to assume that we are in a bubble, I can think of nothing that is further from the truth. It is very early in the Internet of Value. We are redefining what currency is and doing that on a worldwide basis.

Leap into the Quantum Age

What would it have meant to your wealth if you were an early investor in technology companies like Microsoft, Google (Alphabet), Facebook, Netflix or Amazon? Can you see a similarity between early-stage cryptocurrencies and these dominant technology companies?

Chapter 7
The Answers You Need to FAQs

"The world is going digital. People who understand this will make a lot of money. People who don't will miss out on the greatest wealth-building opportunity of our lifetimes."

There is a steep learning curve to understanding crypto and all of the terminology (hence our Glossary of Key Words in the back of the book). Each day, I answer questions from people who want to understand the greatest wealth-building opportunity of our lifetime. Here are some of the frequently asked questions (FAQs) that I receive, and answers to them. I hope this will help clarify things for you.

What Exchanges Can I Buy Cryptocurrencies On?

Cryptocurrencies are bought using apps on your phone. The cryptos below can be found on many exchanges (see CoinMarketCap.com for more), but to keep it simple you can find them on three mentioned here.

These are the apps we use to purchase:

XRP — Uphold, Bitrue (temporarily can't be purchased on Coinbase)

XLM (Stellar Lumens) — Uphold, Coinbase, Bitrue

ALGO (Algorand) — Coinbase

XDC — Bitrue

IOTA — Bitrue

DOGE — Uphold, Coinbase, Bitrue

LTC (Litecoin) — Coinbase, Uphold, Bitrue

FLR (FLARE SPARKS) — Bitrue, later on Uphold and Coinbase

How Can I Buy XRP?

We use the Uphold app to buy XRP. The app is a green color. When you download the Uphold app on your phone from the App Store, you can choose to connect your bank account and buy XRP. Some banks will let you use a debit or credit card to purchase XRP, some won't. Also, it depends on what state and sometimes what country you live in. Go into More, then Linked Accounts. Link your bank account and/or *debit* (not credit) card. Yes, it is OK to give them your Social Security number. It is part of Know Your Customer (KYC) and Anti-Money Laundering (AML) laws.

To move money into your account from your bank, go to Transact. Click the down arrow on From. Choose Banks. Select where you want to move money from. To the left of USD where there is a 0, choose how much money in dollars (or select your currency). For example, $100. Insert an amount. Under "To," touch the down arrow and under Cryptocurrencies, select XRP. It will calculate the amount of XRP you will buy automatically and populate the area. Click Done. Scroll down to Preview Deposit. Click Confirm.

Congratulations, you now own XRP! While you are in the app, you will notice the transfer from "anything to anything" system of currency, stocks and cryptocurrencies is already in existence. Amazing technology.

How Do I Use Coinbase?

The Coinbase app is blue. In Coinbase, go to Settings, then "Add a payment method." Add a bank account or a debit card. I recommend you do not use a credit card. Link your checking account and/or debit (not credit) card as a source of funds. Yes, it is OK to give them your Social Security Number. It is part of Know Your Customer (KYC) and Anti-Money Laundering (AML) laws. Next, at the bottom of the page, touch the round blue button with two horizontal arrows. Then touch Buy crypto with cash. Select XLM or ALGOrand. Touch the "$0" and enter the dollar amount you want to invest. Click "Preview Buy." Click "Buy Now."

Congratulations, you now own crypto!

Is it Safe to Buy XRP and Provide Personal Information?

Some exchanges ask for a photo ID of your driver's license or passport, along with your Social Security Number. Is it safe to give to them? It can be more secure than a bank or credit card, which is vulnerable to hacking and identity theft. Blockchain is actually more secure than current computer storage methods. If you add cold storage, such as the Ledger Nano, your XRP is the most secure. I definitely recommend holding it offline if you can.

Should I Use My Phone or Computer to Set Up My Accounts?

Set up your Uphold account on your phone. Use your computer to transfer XRP to your Ledger Nano or D'CENT wallet if you are going to store it offline (recommended).

How Much Should I Invest?

It is up to you, but don't invest more than you can afford to lose. At this point, it is highly speculative. There are banking regulations that still need to happen. It is possible an exchange can be hacked, and you lose your entire investment. Start slow. Even $100 to $200 could grow into a meaningful amount. Buy the dips, average in and accumulate 1% to 3% of your investable portfolio; then, when you are feeling comfortable, increase your holdings, gradually, to 3% to 5% of your overall investing portfolio (including retirement plans). Try not to chase it, but instead, buy the dips. Volatility is your friend. Consider this a two- to three-year investment.

Think of crypto as a speculation, not an investment. Be cautious and treat it as such. Please do not go overboard or you could seriously hurt yourself. Do not invest more than you can afford to lose. If you don't transfer your XRP from Uphold to the Ledger Nano X or D'CENT wallet, you risk being hacked and could lose everything in your account. You have been warned.

Why is XRP's Price So Low Compared to Bitcoin and Other Cryptos?

I covered this earlier, but to reiterate, one of the things we are watching and waiting for is regulatory clarity. Years ago, bitcoin and Ethereum were given clarity by the SEC that they weren't securities, which allowed investors to buy them and allowed their prices to soar so high. I am hearing rumors that regulatory clarity may be coming for XRP sooner than we think. Some people (like me) believe that regulatory clarity will send XRP much higher.

What we are looking for is referred to as a level playing field. XRP's price has been held down because it doesn't have the regulators saying it is not a security. When U.S. regulators provide clarity that XRP is not a security, it will give legitimacy for XRP to be invested in by large institutions and investment firms. This is a blessing in disguise because we are able to buy XRP at a low price at the moment.

Are Cryptocurrencies Taxed?

Cryptocurrencies are treated as property by the IRS, and they are subject to capital gains and losses rules. This means that when you realize losses after trading, selling or otherwise disposing of your crypto, your losses get deducted from other capital gains, as well as ordinary income (up to $3,000). Please talk to your tax professional for more details.

Crypto exchanges have a downloadable feature that allows you to see a record of all of your trades. Aside from that, Coin Panda is a free software that helps you minimize your taxes and maximize profits. Import your transactions and download crypto tax reports into Coin Panda with the click of a button in under 20 minutes. It supports all popular exchanges and wallets.

What are Stablecoins?

Decentralized Finance (DeFi) refers to the decentralized financial services built on top of distributed blockchain networks with no central intermediaries such as banks, custodians and exchanges. Examples of DeFi protocols include decentralized exchanges (DEXs), decentralized borrowing and lending platforms, and stablecoins, to name a few.

Stablecoins are cryptocurrencies that keep a stable value of one U.S. dollar. Think of it as similar to a non-interest bearing account, although the stablecoin USDC pays a 0.15% interest rate when held in a wallet on Coinbase. From 2020 to 2021, DeFi applications have grown over 20x to $55 billion in total value locked, which is the total amount of assets collateralized with these services.

What is a Privacy Coin?

A privacy coin is a cryptocurrency that is private and anonymous. While people think bitcoin is anonymous, it is not. People can see wallets and how much bitcoin has been transferred in and out of a wallet; they just don't know who it belongs to. With a privacy coin, you see nothing. You don't see how much is moving or where it is going. It is completely anonymous. Just like using cash money, there is no tracing mechanism to a privacy coin. Monero and Ghost coin are privacy coins. Privacy coins cannot be exchanged on a distributed exchange, so they have some limitations. I don't recommend owning or using them.

What Does Trustless Mean?

Trustless means no intermediary is necessary. We are used to having to go through an intermediary to send money. A trustless system means you can send money directly from an app on your phone to an app on a friend's phone without using a bank, money lender or any intermediary. That is because it is not centralized, and no one controls it. That is why many people are speculating that banks will not be needed in 10 years for wiring money, foreign exchange, loans or savings accounts. Perhaps they will be purely investors of money for a fee if they still exist at all.

What are Non-Fungible Tokens (NFTs)?

Non-fungible token is a terribly technical name, but it means a unique digital work. It will probably be used for original music, works of art, photos, video, etc., but anything unique could probably be made into an NFT. Having a grant deed as an NFT would be an awesome application of that technology because an NFT creates that authentic record and individual record. That is why it is not only great for legal documents, but it is also great for artwork, for books, music, for any kind of artistry or any kind of licensing authorship.

You can create a one-of-a-kind work and then people can buy the rights to distribute that work. For example, in the future, a record artist might sell their record to someone as a non-fungible token, and someone can bid for that and buy it, and then they are the distributor. They have the rights to distribute it and maybe make money rather than the record company.

A cool example of that is that artist Beeple, who sold an NFT collage of artworks through auction at Christie's for $69 million. Another example is Jack Dorsey, CEO of Twitter, who made an NFT of his first tweet on Twitter and sold it for $2.9 million. When you hear about something digital selling for $69 million or $2.9 million, it may sound crazy, but maybe there will be ways to replicate it and sell copies or find other uses for it.

Recently, "Saturday Night Live" came up with a comedy piece about NFTs. They made up a rap song about non-fungible tokens and made it look crazy. A lot of times, new technologies are made to look a little bit crazy. That is a strange thing that we have in our culture. But if you look back at when Twitter first came out, people were making fun saying, "Well, what am I supposed to tweet, what I had for breakfast?" And literally, the first tweet I ever read was what somebody ate for breakfast, because they didn't know what to tweet and they didn't know what Twitter was.

More and more companies are coming up with creative ideas for NFTs. *Fortune* magazine is taking 256 of its iconic magazine covers, plus three special editions, and creating NFTs. Coca Cola auctioned its first four NFTs: a digital version of a 1956 Coke vending machine and digital items in a single "loot box" for over $575,000. Marvel Comics is creating an NFT of Spider Man. Other brands are jumping into the fast-growing metaverse. It is only just beginning.

Another use of non-fungible tokens has been among pro-athletes. Basketball greats have sold NFTs of a layup shot or three-pointer that they want memorialized. Music artists will be able to make great use of NFTs with new albums. It will change the game for independent artists, who can auction their records for distribution. They can also connect with their fans by issuing NFTs. Superstar musicians like Kings of Leon and Steve Aoki have already sold NFTs for millions of dollars, while lesser-known musicians Verite and Zack Fox have made tens of thousands of dollars. One artist, Young and Sick, sold an NFT for $865,000, even though he only had 27,000 Instagram followers.

Before this, streaming platforms were how musicians made money, but it didn't pay well: Spotify paid only $.003 to $.005 per stream, which is about $3,000 to $5,000 per 1 million streams; not much for such a large audience. Only 13,400 artists in 2020 generated more than $50,000 (the median wage for U.S. workers) of yearly revenue on Spotify. NFTs will provide an opportunity to make more than they have on streaming platforms. NFTs can also provide recurring revenue, so the artist receives anywhere from 2.5% to 10% of a sale every time the token is resold.

NFTs and cryptocurrencies are even gaining popularity in India, where 15 million people hold around $6.6 billion worth of cryptocurrencies. An Indian musician sold an NFT of a music demo (for limited circulation) for $200,000, which is astonishing.

How Do You Know What to Invest in?

One of the important characteristics of any investment is who is the market leader. In this case, we might say who has the most dominance in the space because it is not just enough to be a first-mover technology. AOL and Yahoo existed before Google, but it was Google that ended up being the dominant search engine. You want to look at dominance — what company is going to dominate the space and be the ultimate leader.

When you are studying technology that you want to invest in, you want to see who is already accumulating relationships with clients and is already the leader in the space. If they get a lead over other companies, they are likely to keep that lead. Not always, but usually that is the one that you want to be investing in. Their growth rate is also important. Companies that are growing the fastest may not be the most profitable, but so far, investors have worried less about profits and more about growth. The stock market has rewarded fast-growing companies, knowing that the profits will come. At least so far, they have, but that could change. You also want to know the management team — what is their experience, what relationships do they have?

Are We Late Getting into Cryptocurrencies?

The high returns are because you are investing early in companies in the next technological revolution, similar to when VCs invest in a company as early-stage investors and are able to enjoy high compounding rates; much higher than we see in the stock market.

One of the top venture capitalists, Andreeson-Horowitz, early investors in companies like Facebook, Twitter, Skype, Lyft, Groupon, AirBnB, and Coinbase is opening up another VC fund and raising $1 billion to invest in cryptocurrency and blockchain technology. I believe this is just the tip of the iceberg. Many more billions will be invested in cryptocurrencies. We will own them first. You are early in the trend and the rates of return are above what everyday investors typically have access to. At this time, only 14% of the population, 21.2 million adults, are invested in cryptocurrency, which means we have a long way to go before this is a bubble. In Chapter 14, I will show you the "12 Anecdotal Signs of a Bubble", so you see what a real asset bubble looks like.

What Can We Compare the Performance of Crypto-currencies to?

We should compare the returns of cryptocurrencies not to stocks, which most people mistakenly do, but to newer companies or start-ups (in terms of rates of return in the thousands of percent) and to currencies (in terms of market capitalization).

Fiat currencies trade $6.6 trillion per day, according to the 2019 Triennial Central Bank Survey of FX and OTC derivatives markets. The foreign exchange (forex market) is the largest financial market in the world (much larger than the stock market) and trades $14.7 billion a day in 2021.

Venture capital is closer to what you are investing in when you invest in a cryptocurrency, blockchain technology companies, smart contracts, DeFi, etc. These are new technologies, and you are investing in them in their early stages. By the time the company goes public, it has already experienced thousands of percent of growth. It may have increased 10,000 times its original valuation. This is not unusual if it is a successful company (obviously, not all are successful). The VCs and insiders then offer their shares to the public in an Initial Public Offering (IPO), where you typically buy the stock as a retail investor – long after the incredible returns have been made. I hope you see how we are turning the tables and getting everyday investors to participate in exponential returns of successful technologies much sooner than you normally would.

What are the Dangers of Crypto?

Like Ripple CEO Brad Garlinghouse said, I believe 90% of cryptocurrencies are probably going to go away when regulations come. That is why we have chosen to invest in ISO 20022 coins. Banks have to plan far in advance and coordinate technology. The ISO cryptos are complying with their regulations. Speculative cryptocurrencies without any utility are the most vulnerable, in my opinion. I think that is obviously something that people need to be aware of. We already know this is a speculative investment, but there are also stories of people getting scammed by email phishing schemes where people pose as being from a company and ask for your passwords or wallet's 24 seed words (like a unique password). Do not give your seed words away for any reason. We also know crypto is highly volatile and as such I have devoted an entire chapter on how to deal with volatility and minimize risk.

Keeping Cryptocurrency Safe

Security against theft in cryptocurrency is much better than you might believe. We have Ledger Nano and D'CENT wallet cold storage offline that we can use to prevent hacking and safely store cryptocurrencies. The Ledger Nano is a small device about the size of a thumb drive that you can buy — you move your cryptocurrency keys onto the Nano and store it completely off the Internet so your cryptocurrency cannot be hacked. You can store multiple cryptos on this device and keep it in your possession. The D'CENT wallet also stores your crypto keys offline and uses your fingerprint to access it.

These methods are the safest way to store cryptocurrency today. You don't want to leave them on an exchange or they could be hacked, although some exchanges store 80% of their cryptos in cold storage and some even insure cryptos against hacking.

I believe the future will eventually be completely digital, but we will have a transition period where physical currency co-exists with digital currency. Is there a circumstance that will hasten cryptocurrencies being used? Yes: It involves the way money works today. Some of its shortcomings are why bitcoin was created in the first place.

You typically buy cryptocurrency through an app on your phone. Not all exchanges offer the same cryptocurrencies. Because they are not all available on one exchange, you will have accounts at multiple exchanges. Some of the exchanges are helpful with storing your cryptos in cold storage off the exchange so if the exchange is hacked, only 10% or 20% of all cryptocurrencies on the exchange are vulnerable at any time. For example, Uphold uses some cold storage and will store 90% of the crypto in their cold storage offline. If a hacker was able to hack their exchange, they could only hack into 10% at any one time. Some exchanges also offer insurance in case the exchange is hacked.

There is always the risk of someone hacking the exchange. If you leave your cryptos on an exchange, you don't have control of your cryptocurrency keys, which is cryptography letters and numbers representing the keys to each crypto, so technically you don't own them. That is why you don't want to leave crypto on an exchange and do want to put it into a Nano or

D'CENT cold storage wallet (best solution) or a hot wallet, which is a software wallet online like Exodus or MEW (apps). Before you invest in a crypto you need to understand where you can store it. For example, at this time the Ledger Nano is not approved to store XinFin (XDC), but the D'CENT wallet is.

The new D'CENT wallet has a biometric element where you have to use a fingerprint to open it. It is also much easier to use than the Ledger Nano, so I have recommended my clients use the D'CENT wallet because the learning curve is not as steep. I have a D'CENT wallet and a Ledger Nano. The best thing to do is be diversified in where you keep your crypto, but you definitely should use a Ledger Nano or D'CENT wallet and store your keys offline if possible. The risk of hacking is a concern you can easily minimize.

How Do I Prevent Getting Scammed?

Never tell people your password or list of seed words. Use two-factor authorization, which is your fingerprint identification with a second method, usually incorporating a number from the Google Authenticator app, which rotates 6 digits that you enter as a second password.

Caution! If you see a tweet that tells you to "send some XRP" to an email address and "more will be sent back to you," it is a *scam* that is seen all over Twitter. They are trying to hack your wallet by getting your email and wallet address. They may even make it look like the request is coming from someone you know. Just ignore it. I highly recommend you get a virtual private network (VPN) if you own any cryptocurrencies. The one I recommend is NordVPN. It can be purchased at NordVPN.com for about $60 annually. A VPN masks your computer activity, protects your online identity and allows you to browse securely. Because we are so early investing in new technology, we are taking extra steps which someday will probably be included, just like when the Internet was brand new, you needed to have security assurances but now have automatic encryption on shopping and payment sites. It is worth it to have peace of mind and the outstanding returns on crypto are worth the relatively small investment in security devices.

Preparing for Quantum Wealth

We have covered a lot of information about cryptocurrencies and other aspects of the Quantum Age. In Part 3 of this book, I would like to share in detail two very important wealth-building tools *that I created that have helped many people — The Wealth Building Formula (McT)™* and the *Six Steps to Wealth.*

Both tools have been in use for multiple years and are very effective. What has changed is that the compounding rates of cryptocurrencies have put the formulas on speed drive, so I have adapted the *Six Steps to Wealth* into the *Three Steps to Quantum Wealth* and put additional emphasis on the compounding aspect of *The Wealth Building Formula (McT)™.* Now that you are familiar with which cryptocurrencies to invest in and why, next we will turn to how you can use them to build and maintain your wealth.

The Bottom Line

Although cryptocurrency can have a steep learning curve, especially if you are not very technologically inclined, it can be done. You have the advantage of a head start. The key is not to give up — stay focused and determined. Pat yourself on the back for becoming aware of an important technological revolution *early.* You can do this!

Leap into the Quantum Age

Be sure to look up any technical terms you don't know in the Key Word Glossary at the back of the book.

Chapter 8
Holding and Trading Strategies

"Trading out of cryptocurrencies has cost people massive fortunes."

Just as Internet stocks became overheated and peaked in 2000, so too will cryptocurrencies and blockchain technologies reach a peak – years from now, in my opinion. Bear markets (a protracted downward-moving market of 20% or more) happen and are necessary to clear out excesses in the market. Markets move from deep pessimism to over-enthusiasm on a regular basis. However, for the astute, bear markets can eventually provide incredible buying opportunities for contrarian investors.

A contrarian investor is someone who goes against the tide and buys when others are selling. While no one likes it when prices and values of investments decline, there is always opportunity that comes with bear markets, as long as you are looking long-term and being strategic about your investing. It won't happen overnight, but if you maintain a long-term focus and are strategic with your buying, you can make some very good investments. As a wise person once said, "A lot of money is made investing in bear markets. You just don't realize it at the time."[19] This is particularly true with stocks and cryptocurrencies.

Each stock represents a business. When a stock market index such as the S & P 500 drops sharply, do all of the companies deserve to drop? Probably not. If there is a recession and profits are going to decline, then of course, some stocks will be worth less. But maybe some companies are declining with the group but shouldn't be. Then you have some gems to buy at a steep discount. This is the market mispricing the value of

---

[19] Shelby Collum Davis, "Wisdom of Great Investors – Quotes", *Davis ETFs website,* https://www.davisetfs.com/investor_education/quotes

companies you can invest in. It is often the best time to invest selectively in quality companies.

How can you plan for a bear market? One way is to watch for signs of speculation and overvaluation. If you are familiar with how to read charts, look for a severely overbought market with a high Relative Strength Indicator (RSI). Look at my list of 12 Signs of a Bubble. Listen for everyone to sound like a crypto investing expert, from the Uber driver to the Starbucks barista. When conversation at cocktail parties among strangers is about stocks, you know you are near a major top in stocks; when it is about cryptocurrencies, you know you are near a major top in cryptos.

Let's say you looked for the speculation and identified it was happening. Then what? If all of the signs are there *and* the market is overbought, then you probably want to take some money off the table. The older you are, the more important that is. Younger people have time to stay in markets, but older people who are retired or near retirement have to be more cautious. It doesn't hurt to take your foot off of the gas and start to brake.

As I have said, about every four years (a four-year cycle), bitcoin and the alt coins — which generally follow bitcoin — move into a bigger correction. It happened in 2013, 2017 and 2021. If that cycle continues, that means 2025 and 2029 will be volatile years for crypto-currencies. However, as cryptocurrencies become more adopted, the cycle highs and lows will tend to even out because they are going mainstream. Because we are getting closer to that point, I do not see 2021 as the end of a cycle. It will be about five years from now before we start seeing the 12 signs in my list.

There are things we will be watching for, but understand that even if we have a bubble peak, such as with the Internet stocks from 2000 to 2002, it doesn't mean these investments are over for good. Did it make sense to sell Amazon in 2002 at $5 and miss the next 20-year run to over $3,000 a share? Nope. Not all cryptocurrencies will survive, but blockchain assets that have invaluable use cases will.

Don't Sell and Withdraw Your Original Investment

It is common trading advice to sell, withdraw the original amount you invested and "play with house money." That is not a good idea when you have a strong compounder. At least not at first. You want to let your winners run and sell your losers.

If you take money out early, you disturb the power of compounding. For example, if you had $1,000 that grew 100% per year for five years, it would grow to $32,000. If instead, you took out $1,000 in year two, you would have $16,000 or 50% less. There is a true story of someone who invested in bitcoin early and paid for a pizza with bitcoin. Because of bitcoin's amazing compounding, later the money spent on the pizza would have been worth *$82 million!* That is one expensive pizza!

I get it: You are itching to buy something. You want to see something tangible for the investing success you've had. You want to buy a new car or a beach house. You want something to show for it. You have things you want to do. Now that you have the money, you are itching to spend it. Let me ask you a question: Would you sell the golden goose to buy a depreciating asset? Would you sell what makes you money to buy a car that will be worth half its value in about three years? Or sell your cash flow to build a swimming pool? Would you turn off a flowing faucet of money to go on a trip or buy a second home?

You have to think about the long-term consequences of short-term passions on spending your investment principal. Is it worth it? Will you regret it? There are those who say "take profits!" I get it. Many times, big gains go away, and you have nothing to show for them. You might be fearful that may happen. But you have to balance your decisions and watch your investments closely.

Let's look at what happens if you withdraw money early when compounding wealth. You start with $1,000 and it grows to $3,000. Let's compare what happens over 10 years if you remove your original $1,000 investment when it is compounding at 15% annually. If you invested $3,000 x 15% compounded x 20 years = $49,099. But if you took your original $1,000 out of the

$3,000 and compounded $2,000 x 15% x 20 years, it would equal only $32,733 — a $16,000 difference! *The higher the compounding rate, the more costly the mistake is.* It can cost you dearly.

Compounding is the most crucial step of the *Six Steps to Wealth*. It is important to earn the highest rate you can without withdrawing any funds from the investment. If you make the mistake of withdrawing money from the account in the early years, it will set back your wealth-building. For example, if you invested $100,000 for 30 years at 10%, you would have $1,744,940, but if you withdrew $20,000 in year five, you would only have $1,027,827. In other words, the $20,000 withdrawal really cost you $717,113.

Am I saying you can never sell? How do you enjoy the fruits of the wealth created? I hear that all the time. People don't understand an important concept: You don't kill the goose laying the golden eggs. If you take money out of your best investment, you are killing the golden goose. People stop the money spigot because they want to spend it. There is also fear of losing the money and that the profits will disappear, especially because crypto is so volatile. But if you sell, then you have to decide when to buy back in, so you really have two decisions to get right.

You might think $3 million is so much money it will last you forever. But after taxes, gifts to family, houses, cars, jewelry, trips, college tuition, etc., it goes pretty fast. Yes, it is possible to spend that much and run out of money. If you spend principal and don't replenish the funds because you killed the golden goose, you have one foot on a slippery slope to going through the money fast.

As I said, you want to keep your best investments and sell your worst performers. Unfortunately, most people do the opposite. They sell their best performers and keep the worst. Again, you have stopped the compounding at a high rate. Not good.

Crypto Trading Strategies

Many investors have the attitude, "Take some profits along the way." They want to try to time the market, selling at highs and hoping to buy the investment back at a lower price. However, they really don't understand how that is detrimental to their wealth-building.

An interesting true story is one of the early investors in bitcoin. He wanted to see what it was like to use bitcoin as a currency, so he bought a pair of socks with a couple of hundred bitcoins. It turns out if he had kept the bitcoins, today they would have been worth millions of dollars.

I see people "taking profits" and selling their cryptocurrencies for pennies. That is a huge mistake. Do you really think the all-time high is going to be $0.39 cents? David Schwartz, the Chief Technology Officer of Ripple, said on Twitter that he made a mistake and sold Ethereum for a $42,000 gain. He meant to buy it back but didn't. He lamented that *had he kept his Ethereum, it would be worth $90 million!* Ouch. This can be a problem when you are trying to time the market. Yes, you can sell for a profit, but like David, many people forget to buy back in and miss the life-changing wealth.

People have regrets about selling bitcoin or Dogecoin at $0.30. How they could have thought this was as valuable as it would ever get is beyond me. Maybe they weren't educated about what they were buying and they listened to the fear, uncertainty and doubt (FUD).

While taking profits and trading in and out of XRP sound great, the reality is much more difficult. There is no clear guide to that, and you can be out of the market and miss getting back in at the right time. More worrisome is that many exchanges have removed the buy button for XRP and made it impossible to buy because of the lawsuit. We are fortunate to have purchased it on Uphold, where it is still available.

Investing in XRP is different from investing in a stock or real estate. This is a currency, an asset that won't be negatively affected by inflation. It can be used for payments, tokenized investments and money in the future. Why would you want to go back into fiat currency? You won't have to cash XRP in. You can stake it and earn interest. Flare Sparks are giving you five ways to earn passive income and in the long term, it is still likely to increase in value.

My plan is to hold XRP for years, knowing I never have to sell (or pay taxes on gains). If I hold, I won't miss buying back in, and it won't ever have to be converted into anything else since it is a currency. You can choose your own path, but that is my plan and what I recommend for our VIPs. The most value I can offer VIP members is to instill confidence in times when they feel fearful. I am there to remind them of the big picture and to hold for the long term. Many have told me that before being a VIP, they would panic and sell. Now they hold on confidently through the volatility.

One day after extreme volatility in XRP, I posted this in our private VIP Facebook group to strengthen their resolve to hold through the dip:

"This is how the trading bots try to shake you out. They have an algorithm where the price soars, then drops, then soars. The second time it soars, they want you to get out and lock in your profits. Then it repeats higher, and you are out, and the price is too much higher to buy back in. It is not easy to stay calm unless you really understand what you own and how valuable it is. Your own fear of losing money, fear of poverty, fear of it not being real, are what you have to overcome to make it to the finish line. This is a marathon, not a sprint. Prepare for one to two years of wild fluctuations. If you can do that (and I know you can), you just might experience avalanches of abundance!"

Some people really want to try to take profits and sell some of their positions high and then buy back low. You could take 25% of your holdings and do that by looking at charts and seeing where we are in the channel. However, there is still the chance that you don't buy back in and the 25% misses out on dramatic highs. Or worse, you sell it all to take profits and don't buy it back.

For example, this is a real tweet from someone who traded bitcoin (we are using bitcoin as an example. XRP is following in its tracks, but it is a few years behind). He said: "I wish I had kept my 1,700 BTC @ $0.06 instead of selling them at $0.30, now that they are $8.00!" That was tweeted in May 2011. Here he was lamenting he missed out on $13,600. In 2021, his bitcoins grew *to be worth $63,000 each. If he had held on to his 1,700 bitcoins, today they would be worth $107 million!* That is the problem with trying to trade a dominant winner like bitcoin or, I believe, XRP. In the end, wouldn't it have been wiser for him just to hold through the volatility?

Strategy Tips and Mindset during Pullbacks

Fluctuations are emotional and can cause panic. However, when you understand what you own, why you own it and that you are investing in the trend very early, you can feel some comfort through the wild swings up and down. Because cryptocurrencies move so much on the upside, they also move a lot to the downside. It is not usual for something to go up 300% or more and also drop 60% in the same year. However, if you can keep a long-term perspective and keep your emotions in check, you will find compounding rates beyond anything available in the stock market, potentially building wealth faster and shaving decades off the time it would take with a stock.

It is important to frame pullbacks and dips correctly. This is what you should *not* do:

- Feel scared and wonder what happened? What's wrong?

- Panic, thinking the move is over.

- Lose faith in the reasons you made the investment in the first place.

- Kick yourself for investing.

What you *should* do:

- Realize after a big move up, a pullback is normal and expected. That is how all markets work.

- Understand that pullbacks are temporary on the long-term climb upward to life- changing wealth.

- Reaffirm in your mind why all of the reasons you decided to make this investment still exist and that the creator of XRP said it was designed to run at much higher prices for ease of use.

- Remember the fact that "bull markets climb a wall of worry," meaning strong upward trends require you to feel scared and worried that they have ended or will end.

- Keep a long-term perspective and HODL! (Hold On for Dear Life).

Dollar Cost Averaging is Your Friend

Buy the dips. That means when crypto goes down, that is when you should buy, not while it is skyrocketing up. Chelsea could have bought XRP for $0.25. She waited and hesitated until it started going up dramatically. She ended up buying close to a top and paying over $1.50. After that, it pulled back to around $0.40. She would have been better off buying the dips than chasing the run-up. With dollar cost averaging, you can buy using the same dollar amount at regular intervals, just like when you invest in your 401(k) every month. That is one way. Another way is to buy the dips. I prefer to buy the dips.

Investors fear they are going to miss out and the price is going to run away forever and never pull back. The reality is computer algorithms control much of the professionals trading today and as I have explained, psychology went into determining how to manipulate our emotions so they can take advantage. The only way I see we can beat them is to buy and hold our crypto in cold storage, such as on a Ledger Nano or D'CENT wallet.

Investing in Disruptive Technology is Profitable

One topnotch hedge fund manager has noticed the returns and announced he would be investing in cryptocurrencies in the near future. He said, "I'm doing a deep dive into crypto. I'm fully converted." He went on to say, "Forget bitcoin. I don't care about bitcoin. I care more about the technology behind the blockchain and how transformational it is and how disruptive it could be."[20]

According to Clayton M. Christensen, a Harvard Business School professor, a disruptive technology is a new, emerging technology that unexpectedly displaces an established one.[21] Disruption is the ultimate when looking at potential returns in new technology. Being a disruptive technology means it can become dominant in its usage and huge in scale. Past examples of disruptive technologies would include electricity, the automobile, the television, fast food. More contemporary examples include personal computers, email, e-commerce, social media and ride-sharing.

A prominent venture capital firm said, *"We believe that the next wave of computing innovation will be driven by crypto,"* and that they are *"radically optimistic about crypto's potential."* They just raised $2.2 billion in their third round of crypto investments. It is the world's largest crypto fund to date.[222]

The Bottom Line

Be a patient investor. Think about the long-term gains that an investment with high compounding rates like crypto can create. Don't be quick to sell or try to time getting in and out of the market. We are investing so early it is best to buy and hold.

---

[20] Steven A. Cohen, https://news.bitcoin.com/billionaire-steve-cohen-deep-dive-into-crypto-fully-converted-not-missing-this/?fbclid=IwAR0Xy7C9jiOUBTe79EYk7BDurKbCCKD bp0t4DzEkJUfJ-WLcXaaQkOQp8

[21] https://www.technologyhq.org/guide-12-disruptive-technology-examples/

[22] Kate Rooney, CNBC.com, 6/24/21, https://www.cnbc.com/2021/06/24/andreesen-horowitz-launches-2point2-billion-crypto-fund.html

Leap into the Quantum Age

1. Notice where interest rates are and what direction
    they are moving. If they are at an extreme low, what
    direction might they move next? How might that
    affect your investments?

2. Chances are at least once in your life you chose not
    to invest in something and missed a wealth-building
    opportunity. What were you feeling at that point?
    Perhaps you meant to invest and did not, or you
    invested and sold too soon. What were you thinking
    and feeling? What would you do differently so you
    don't make the same mistake? What or who will help
    you not make the same mistake again?

3. Are you willing to lock up part of your crypto
    investments for years? What is your crypto strategy
    — trade, sell along the way, or buy and hold?

Chapter 9
Asset Allocation and Risk

"Investing requires that you tolerate fluctuating investment values. Holding steadfast is the sign of a good investor."

I think risk has gotten a bad rap.

Risk is really "fluctuation." Some people have a hard time with their investment accounts fluctuating. Many times, I have found this is a mindset problem. They are full of fear that they will lose all of their money, so they panic and sell when their account is down.

What they fail to understand is all investments fluctuate in value. Your home fluctuates in value. Gold and silver fluctuate in value. Bonds fluctuate in value. Because an investment fluctuates more on the upside, it is also likely to fluctuate more on the downside. In other words, better investments can have wilder swings in value. This is not for the faint of heart. You have to have a lot of confidence in what you own to hold it confidently through the swings and drops.

A Lower Risk Tolerance Means Limiting Your Upside Potential

I think the investment industry has done a disservice to clients by making them think fluctuation is the same as risk. It is common for financial institutions to ask clients how much fluctuation they can stand. If a client says they don't like it, the institution gives them a "less risky" portfolio. What that really means is they are limiting the upside potential of that portfolio. If bonds don't fluctuate as much as stocks and also earn 40% less on average, then by saying you want less fluctuation, you are saying you want a lower annual return. That means less compounding, and ultimately less money in your retirement account. Is that what you want when you say you want less fluctuation?

Cryptocurrency is the most volatile asset I have ever invested in. It is much more volatile than Internet stocks were, and I thought those were volatile. They don't hold a candle to the swings in crypto! It can be exhilarating to experience your money doubling quickly. I've never experienced anything like this.

When you consider the upward moves in cryptocurrencies in one year, of course it is going to have downside fluctuations, too. Investments that are volatile on the upside have traders who are constantly trading on the up and down moves. As we talked about in the last chapter, that doesn't mean *you* have to. Quite the contrary, I encourage you to do your homework about why you own something, and then hold it through the ups and downs. As Warren Buffett said, *"The stock market is a device for transferring money from the impatient to the patient."*[23] Many people get impatient if their investment doesn't start climbing immediately.

Being able to have confidence in the midst of fluctuation of value is the most important trait to have as an investor. Digital assets are much more volatile than stocks, but that makes sense, because the returns are so much higher. If $1,000 can grow to $300,000 in five years, do you think it is because it is easy? Do you think it is because everyone and anyone will be able to stay confident while the crypto price acts like a bucking bronco? Not likely.

Unless you have a firm understanding of what you are invested in and why, and strong support to keep you holding, you may fold, even if you have a winning hand like a royal flush of digital assets. People lose confidence in their ideas when value declines. It gives them FUD — fear, uncertainty and doubt. They start to doubt their decisions because they don't see the market price confirming their decision that it is a good investment. They

---

[23] Warren Buffet, *Quora,* https://www.quora.com/What-does-Buffet-mean-when-he-says-the-stock-market-is-a-device-for-transferring-money-from-the-impatient-to-the-patient

think "I was wrong" or worse, "I made a mistake," simply because of the fluctuating price.

This has nothing to do with you being right or wrong. The market is driven by algorithms that are trading bots, designed to discourage humans from holding on. Hedge funds hire psychologists to study human emotions. They know how to drive a price up and then drop it hard to evoke panic. This allows them to make money in both directions, whether crypto is going up or down. You have to know what you own and have confidence in what you invested in to stay the course!

How Asset Allocation Model Questionnaires Work

Asset allocation is very similar among financial institutions. Accepting a "high level of risk" means you are able to deal with wide fluctuations in the value of your portfolio. That means they can invest your money in an "aggressive" manner, which is a greater percentage in stocks, which will compound at the highest rate. If you indicate you are a "moderate" risk-taker, then you are saying you want less money in stocks and more in bonds (which earn almost nothing in today's interest rate environment), so you are severely hampering your growth potential.

Asset allocation is very similar whether you are at ABC brokerage or XYZ brokerage. Advisors are taught to diversify you the same way. They recommend you own a portion of your portfolio in large company stocks (large caps), medium company stocks (mid caps), small company stocks (small caps), international companies, smaller international companies known as emerging markets, real estate investment trusts and bonds. They slice up your portfolio into pieces of each and charge you an annual fee of 1.5 to 2% annually on top of the fees in the investments (like ETFs or mutual funds).

An aggressive portfolio might have 80% in stocks, while a moderate portfolio might have 60% in stocks. The balance is in bonds or income-producing vehicles, which sounds good, but compound at a much lower rate. As I said, the average long-term return on stocks is roughly 10% and the average long-term return on bonds is likely to be very limited. Why? Because interest rates are at all-time lows, and they can only go in one direction: up. When interest rates go up, bond values decline, so the bond market is not where you want to be putting a large portion of your money.

Some will argue with that and say it is a "stabilizing" part of a portfolio, but in actuality, it is a way to earn almost nothing on 20% or 40% of your portfolio. There was a time when you could rely on a 6% to 8% return on bonds and they made sense in a portfolio; however, those days are gone. The new reality is they are a drag on your returns, and you need to be wise to that or you will hamper your growth and journey to financial freedom.

The Old 60/40 Stock/Bond Model is Dead

The income portion of a portfolio used to be higher income-generating so you had some cushion of income. For decades, the financial industry asset allocation model was 60% stocks, 40% bonds. That made sense when you were earning an 8% annual return on bonds, but then interest rates declined to near zero, making 40% of your portfolio earn only about 1% to 3%. In the "old days," when interest rates were 6% to 8% on average, you earned a healthy amount of interest. That is no longer the case, but unfortunately, many asset allocation models are still 60% stocks and 40% bonds. That could be drastically hurting your average compounding rate of return.

My Growth Asset Allocation Model

I like having some money invested in large companies (large caps or large capitalization companies, like in the S & P 500); mid caps (medium-size companies or mid-capitalization); and small caps (small companies or small capitalization). The building blocks of a portfolio are having some money in large caps, mid caps, small caps, Real Estate Investment Trusts (REITs), international companies (outside the U.S.), and emerging market companies (up-and-coming markets such as Brazil, Russia, India, China and South Africa). I like to add some baskets of fast-growing technologies such as electric cars, cryptocurrencies, electric batteries and medicinal cannabis that have high long-term growth rates and give you the potential to have higher compounding rates for years to come.

That is why I structured investments differently. I created a growth portfolio that addresses the compounding portion. It is up to you how much growth you want to own. If you want 80% of your money in growth, you are free to choose that. The other 20% would be up to you to decide how to allocate for cash/savings/safety. It could be divided among a savings account, dividend paying stocks, REITs, MLPs, etc. You can also choose bonds or a money market, but those returns are near zero because interest rates are so low. That is why I leave it up to you where to put the income or cash portion.

Choose the portion of your portfolio to invest in growth. If you choose 70%, then 70% of your portfolio would go into this model. The other 30% would be your choice of income/cash vehicles, such as dividend-paying stocks, REITs, MLPs, or now interest-bearing crypto. Again, you can also choose bonds, a savings account or a money market, but on that portion of your portfolio, the rates of return are likely to be near zero because interest rates are so low.

For example, a basic growth asset allocation model may look like this:

Large cap value and large cap growth, 21%

Mid cap value and mid-cap growth, 11%

Small cap value and small cap growth, 9%

Real Estate Investment Trusts (REIT), 3%

International, 6%

Emerging Markets, 2%

Specialty Sector ETFs (multiple), 3% to 5% each

Cryptocurrency, 3% to 5%

One of the reasons we are invested in a specialty ETF involved in the electric car industry is because electric cars are expected to grow at an annualized rate of 40% per year until

2027, which could double corporate profits in less than two years. Other favorite sectors I have shared on the podcast include large gold and silver mining stocks, junior gold and silver mining stocks, and medicinal cannabis. Of course, most 401(k) menus only have the basic asset classes (the first six above), but you can open a brokerage account and invest in the specialty ETFs. As you know, cryptocurrencies are invested in through apps on your phone.

By using diversification this way, the portfolio is broadly diversified and not too heavy in any one ETF. Since ETFs can fluctuate more, this helps to minimize swings. But we know that more fluctuation is likely to be on the downside and upside when investing in cryptocurrencies.

Cryptocurrencies are not correlated to stocks. That means when stocks go up, they may or may not be going up, too, and when stocks go down, cryptos may or may not be going down at the same time. They usually aren't. That is why crypto is the perfect asset class to have as a complement to a stock portfolio, in my opinion.

The way our asset allocation model is constructed has been called a "core and satellite" investing style. It means you have your core portfolio in small, mid- and large cap stocks; REITs; and international and emerging markets. They are your "core" holdings. The smaller "satellite" holdings are the specialty ETFs and crypto.

Investing is Not Gambling

Some people confuse gambling and investing. Gambling is a guess that will be 100% right or wrong. It is an all-or-nothing proposition. Investing, if done correctly, is gathering information about the past and the future that gives you enough knowledge to decide about what will prosper in the future.

If you don't do your homework and you randomly invest because someone gave you a tip, you are acting like a gambler, not an investor. If you do your homework to learn about the company, study its financials, see how competitive it is in the marketplace, learn about the growth prospects of the sector it is in, investigate its management team, look at charts of the stock price, and — most importantly — monitor its profitability and growth prospects, you are an investor.

There are a lot of tools that can help you do the work yourself, or you can subscribe to a service that does the research for you. Anyone can plug ETFs into an asset allocation model that will get fair market returns (and you don't have to pay a financial advisor fees to do it), but looking for specialty growth is a little more challenging. You want to have some ability for your portfolio to outperform the indexes and that can be very expensive with a traditional financial advisor, to the tune of 1% to 3% of your assets annually to do so (if you have a portfolio under $1 million, the total fees may be higher). On a million-dollar portfolio, that is $10,000 to $30,000 paid to an advisor per year in fees.

Are You Being Kept Informed?

When you are trusting expert advice, it is most important that you are kept updated. It is important for you to know what is going on in the stock and crypto markets and be updated about your portfolio. The information should be delivered to you; you shouldn't have to call and ask for it. It can be something as simple as a short summary you can read in 5 to 15 minutes once a month, with a review of every investment in your portfolio and the markets.

Investing in the S & P 500 is about diversifying among different asset classes and identifying high compounding trends that will continue for years to come. Knowing that medical cannabis companies are compounding, as a group, at a 35% rate for the next five years is intriguing, for instance.

We are in the Quantum Age when so much is changing. Legacy energy (oil) is changing to green energy. Legacy cars (gas guzzlers) are shifting to electric vehicles. Companies going public are using one of our digital asset companies, Algorand, to create a tokenized version of the stock. Rather than just being able to buy the stock on the stock market through your stock brokerage, you can already invest in stocks like Microsoft, Apple and Amazon on the Uphold app, a cryptocurrency exchange. And you can exchange anything for it — foreign currencies, dollars, crypto, precious metals, stablecoins or other stocks. There are already 50 stocks and nine ETFs with a digital representation on Uphold. Soon, the entire S & P 500 will be digitized, trading on digital exchanges, 24 hours a day, with instant settlement. We are not far from that now. The transition is underway.

The Bitwise 100 Largest Cryptocurrency Index

We use indexes like the S & P 500 to judge performance. There is one index of cryptocurrencies called the Bitwise Index. It is a private placement (not for public investment; again, accredited investors only), a basket of the top 100 largest cryptocurrencies. The five-year performance is 6,000%! If we used this number to calculate our rate of compounding going forward, it is mind boggling, yet this is exactly what we do with stock indexes.

This is past performance, which is no guarantee of future results, however, it is *real past performance.* The fact that cryptocurrencies have astronomical rates of return to-date is real, not imaginary. I believe they can continue to be achieved for some period of time. At some point, the returns will have to come down, but we may have years of high returns first. As I have demonstrated, small businesses can realistically grow at 1,000% or more for at least the first several years. In the future, many investors who own cryptocurrencies will become millionaires and billionaires. I can say that because I believe the high compounding rates will continue for many years. While cryptocurrency compounding rates have decreased the time needed to create wealth, very few investors are benefiting. With only 14% of the population owning any cryptos at all, we need to get the word out.

The Bottom Line

Knowledge is power. To create investments that build wealth, you need to create a diversified portfolio built on a strong market knowledge and a strong mindset.

Leap into the Quantum Age

It's time to take the leap. If you haven't invested in cryptocurrency, consider investing 5% of your portfolio, but only if you have the risk tolerance to hold for the long-term through volatile short-term price swings.

Section Three

The Three Steps to Quantum Wealth

"By 2024, at least half of the world's population is expected to use digital wallets for transactions that will be valued at more than $9 trillion annually."

— Ripple.com

Chapter 10

The Wealth Building Formula (McT)™

"Wealth-building is simply a function of how much money you
have, what rate you can compound it at and for how long –
and then becoming certain that it will happen."

Whether you are new to investing or a seasoned investor,
I believe that you will find the *Wealth Building Formula (McT)*™
a useful tool to make it easy to understand the components of
wealth-building and how to make up for any shortfalls or
challenges you have on your way to attaining financial freedom.

For example, what if, like 45% of Americans, you have
$0 saved for retirement? What if you are now 60? You know from
the *Wealth Building Formula (McT)*™ that you have challenges
in the M and T areas. What can you do? There is only one answer.
It has to be compounding (c) at a high rate. That is why you need
to consider investing a small portion of your portfolio in
cryptocurrencies.

If you are earning a low rate of return because your
money is stashed in a low-yielding savings account (which is a
common mistake), you have a low compounding rate (c) and will
have to make up for it by adding more money (M) or investing
for a longer time (T). This means you may have to put off
retirement or your financial goal. Of course, the higher your rate
of compounding (c), the faster you will build wealth and the less
money you will need to invest. In effect, it is the magic bullet.
Cryptocurrencies have such high compounding rates that even a
small amount invested in them can create a big improvement
(and, as you will soon see, perhaps even "crazy wealth") in your
portfolio.

If you are lacking one of the three parts, such as not
having much money (M) to invest, you can make up for it by

expanding the other factors, (c) and (T). For example, to make up for a lack of money, you will need to invest and get high compounding rates (c) or invest for a longer time (T) in years. Likewise, if you started investing late in life and you needed to make up for a lack of years or time (T) to reach your goal, you would need to add more money (M) or invest at higher compounding rates (c).

Since the three factors M, c and T work together, a shortage of one or more is going to create obstacles for you to overcome. Based on this formula, people usually have at least one of the following limitations that make it challenging to build wealth and reach a financial goal.

M — Not enough money to invest. This is when you are challenged by not having enough money; for example, if your retirement accounts and other savings don't come close to $100,000 or more to invest.

C — Not investing well. You may have a good nest egg saved and more than 10 years until retirement, but your investments are compounding at low rates of return or worse, like 53% of Americans, your money is sitting idle in a savings account earning almost nothing.

T — Not enough time (years). You got a late start with investing, and you do not have many years to reach your financial goal or until retirement. If you have fewer than 10 years to grow your wealth, it can be a big challenge because having fewer years stunts the compounding effect.

In addition, people may not have enough certainty that they can invest. Less than 29% of women see themselves as investors according to a study by Fidelity. I find some people don't even make an effort to learn how to invest because they don't believe they can learn it or succeed. Sadly, they have given up without even trying. I hope this book changes that.

Before we get into specifics about the *Wealth Building Formula (McT)*™, I want to share something with you. Recently,

Claris Finance[24] did a survey that asked Americans about their worst money mistakes. Common mistakes were not paying off credit card debt, not saving at all, incurring debt on unnecessary purchases, and lacking financial responsibility early in life. But there was one money mistake that 23% of Americans said was their worst. Can you guess what it was? Yep, not saving enough from monthly income.

We all try to save money, but living is expensive. You are smart and may even have your income automated to put extra money into savings or an emergency savings fund. But there is something important that many people are missing that can overcome insufficient savings, especially for retirement savings. The big variable is the "c" — compounding.

We are going to review the real returns of our recommended cryptocurrencies that we believe have dominant technology to be the big winners in the future – and as you will see, in the last five years they certaintly have started out exceeding our wildest expectations!

Better Compounding is the Answer

What rate of return are you compounding your money at? It makes a *huge* difference to your retirement and life. The better your investments do, the sooner you can reach your financial goals and the more money you will have to spend in retirement and in life. Getting your investments to work harder for you will make up for any lack in your plan. The answer is better compounding, and cryptocurrencies provide the best opportunity for superior rates of return. For example, let's compare three investment choices: a savings account, stocks and cryptos.

- If you invest $10,000 per year for retirement and earn only 2% interest, in a savings account (quite a generous rate today), you will have $262,692 after 20 years (with $200,000 total invested) and after 30 years ($300,000 total invested) would grow to $431,908.

---

[24] *MoneyWise*, Claris Finance study of 2,000 Americans, 2018.
https://moneywise.com/life/entertainment/biggest-financial-regrets

- If instead you invest in the stock market and it averages its historical rate of return of 10% annually, $10,000 invested per year over 20 years ($200,000 total invested) would grow to $697,299 and in 30 years ($300,000 total invested) would grow to $1,983,928.

- If you could invest $10,000 per year into a cryptocurrency that averaged 60% for 6.5 years, it would grow to $751,461. In effect, you have shortened the time to accumulate more than $700,000 from 20 years (invested in stocks) to 6.5 years by investing in cryptocurrency, shaving off more than a decade, or 13.5 years. You also saved $135,000 you didn't have to invest. That is a huge amount of money and time saved from a small amount invested and a relatively short period of time to invest. *That* is the power of compounding at high rates. Cryptocurrencies are the ultimate high-compounding investment.

M = Money or How Much You Have to Invest

Let's expand on M — the amount of money you have. You do not have to have a lot of money to get started. In fact, it doesn't really matter how much you have. It is more important that you do something with whatever you have. Even making one good decision can change your financial circumstances, so it is important to act.

Years ago, when I started investing in stocks, I did not feel I had enough money, and I certainly did not feel like I knew enough. I lacked confidence and was scared I was going to lose money. But over time, I was pleasantly surprised at how quickly I could recover from mistakes and get back on course. That helped develop my confidence, as did writing down my investment account balance daily. By tracking it every day, I was monitoring my money closely. Ignoring money is the kiss of death.

C = Compounding or Your Rate of Return

As I mentioned, compounding is wealth-building. Compounding is simply growing your money in whatever money engine you choose, whether it is a stock, bond, real estate, crypto, business or other means. It is the interest rate part of the calculation derived from your investment. What you are actually doing is taking your income and investing it in a growing asset that is building wealth for you.

You want to have assets on your net-worth statement that will increase in value, not depreciate. I have talked about stocks and cryptocurrencies compounding at a much higher rate than a savings account. As you know, the benefit of that is you are building wealth faster.

The S & P 500 stock index returned 15% for the last five years instead of the longer-term average of 10%. Therefore, your $100,000 grew into $201,135 in five years instead of $161,051. That is a good thing. Anytime you can compound your money better, you are reaching or exceeding your goals faster.

To take advantage of superior compounding rates, what makes sense is making smart choices and diversifying a small portion of your portfolio, just like Goldman Sachs, Morgan Stanley Private Wealth, Yale and Harvard Endowments are doing. They are investing 5% of their portfolios in cryptocurrencies and blockchain technology. That is what I recommend you do, too. You can see how only a small investment can grow into a meaningful amount with cryptocurrencies. You don't have to be taking big risks. A small investment will serve you well.

How Have Our Recommended Cryptocurrencies Performed?

Because the Quantum Age technology we are talking about has higher compounding rates of return than any other asset class in history, the returns of many cryptocurrencies are in the hundreds or thousands of percent. Here are how our recommended cryptocurrencies performed year-to-date through September 12, 2021, and for the last five years.

YTD Return		5-year Return[25]
XRP:	367%	18,787%
XLM:	140%	17,048%
ALGO:	598%	- 13%
XDC:	2,049%	20,361%
IOTA:	402%	222%
DOGE:	5,270%	107,650%
LTC:	43%	4,675%
FLR:	264% (not issued yet, this is an IOU value on the Bitrue exchange).	

That means if you invested $1,000 five years ago in all seven (excluding FLR, which is brand-new), your money would have grown to $187,870 in XRP; $170,480 in XLM; $987 in ALGO; $203,610 in XDC; $2,220 in IOTA; $1,076,500 in Dogecoin; and $46,750 in LTC.

Wait, whaaaat?

That's right: Your $7,000 investment would have grown to $1,688,417 in 5 years!

These are real returns. While it is incredible to see these returns, we cannot count on the next five years having the same performance. This is highly unlikely to repeat these rates of compounding. We need to keep a level head. Sound investing principles are still important, even when the compounding returns (c) are off the charts, so we will continue on with our examples, as if we had more traditional and subdued compounding rates of return.

Unlike the stock market returns during the pandemic, these incredible returns do not have anything to do with Covid-induced shortages, like we have seen with housing, highly shorted stocks and lumber. These returns are from being early in the cycle, early in the technology (almost venture capital stage) and owning a completely new asset class that is unique.

---

[25] *CoinCodex website,* YTD through September 12, 2021, https://coincodex.com

T = Time or Start Investing as Early as Possible

Besides the compounding rate, time (T) is also important. Time is the number of years you have to invest — how many years you can compound your money. Do you have 10 or 30 years to invest? The function of time is important because the longer you can invest, the more you can compound money. Having more time means you have more years to allow the magic of compounding to work for you. That is why it is extremely important to start investing as soon as possible.

Age 40 to 45 is usually when retirement saving needs to become serious. Recently, I was talking to someone I just met, and she was telling me her concerns about getting a late start on saving for her retirement. She was in her mid-40s and was really starting to panic that she hadn't really saved enough for retirement. While I agreed with her that she hadn't saved enough, I also knew that because of her age, she still had a pretty good amount of time to save and compound money for retirement.

Under current law, workers who are age 45 today have to work until age 70, an increase from the past retirement age of 65. They can choose to receive reduced benefits at age 62. The government's solution to retirement is having you work longer and retire later. While that is one option, that it not necessarily the right option for everyone, especially for people who really want to retire sooner.

At age 43, this person still has 25 to 30 years for compounding to work for her. Time is on her side, but this is the time to get after it because this is where she still has an advantage of a lot of time (T) in years to compound, but time is quickly slipping away. Once you get to under 25 years, the compounding is not as dramatic. The longer she waits to start, the more she will have to compensate with more money (M) invested or higher compounding rates (c). Fortunately, even a small amount like 5% invested in cryptocurrencies may provide a big boost to an investment portfolio.

Of course, you can save more money, and the older you are, the more money you should be putting aside. I talked about that in my *Wealth Heiress* book, where people got a late start but made catch-up contributions to their IRAs. They were able to put more money aside and catch up because they were also investing well and compounding at a high rate. Compounding involves being a good investor and not having your money sit in a savings account earning 1% interest.

If you are investing in your 401(k) and using a standard asset allocation model for investing in the S & P 500, mid-caps (medium-sized companies), small caps (small companies), international, emerging markets, perhaps real estate and some of your favorite sectors, that kind of a portfolio is going to get you to higher compounding rates potentially. You saw my asset allocation model for stocks and cryptocurrencies in chapter 9.

Certainly, the earlier you start saving for retirement, the less stressful it is going to be on you and the less money you are going to have to put aside. I often use the example of investing $5,000 a year at 10% (which is a good average stock market return over the long term) and a 40-year compounding period. Someone who can compound $5,000 a year for 40 years at 10% will end up with $2.6 million. The reason that example is so powerful is mainly because of the time factor: We are using 40 years as a compounding factor.

Let's change that a bit and take $5,000 contributed to an IRA for 30 years at the same 10% rate. We are still assuming that you're investing well and getting long-term stock market returns, but you started 10 years later and have 30 years to invest. Well, $5,000 invested for 30 years at 10% would equal $991,000. The same amount of money that earns the same return but starting 10 years later is going to get you under $1 million, instead of $2.6 million. Do you see how the time factor affects how much you have at retirement?

Let's look at it this way. Say you doubled your contribution from $5,000 a year to $10,000 a year for 30 years and earned the same 10% return. It wouldn't grow to $2.6 million even if you doubled your contributions, because your time factor is still 10 years shorter. So instead of $2.6 million like the first example, if you've doubled your contributions from $5,000 to

$10,000 a year and compound it for 30 years at 10%, it will equal $1.9 million.

Now remember that you've paid in $150,000 more — $5,000 a year times 30 years. That's $150,000 extra you have paid in, and you still have $700,000 less than if you started 10 years earlier. Clearly, time (T) is one of the most valuable factors of the three factors (money, compounding and time) in the *Wealth Building Formula (McT)™*. That is why it is so important for you to get started saving and investing as early as you possibly can.

Because the average compounding rates are so high on cryptocurrencies, it is changing the McT equation in your favor. In the next chapter, I'm going to show you how to reduce the *Six Steps to Wealth* into *Three Steps to Quantum Wealth*. One of the things I really believe is that your mindset is the foundation of all wealth and the biggest determinant as to whether or not you can attain and maintain financial freedom. That is why it is so important to address your mindset for wealth before talking about what to invest in.

The Bottom Line

Formulas can change the world. Just ask Einstein about $E=mc^2$. Obviously, I'm not Einstein, but I do believe that applying the *Wealth Building Formula (McT)™* can change your life.

Leap into the Quantum Age

Consider taking small amounts of money and buying on days when the price dips. Then hold on for dear life (HODL)!

Chapter 11

Step One to Quantum Wealth: Set a Certainty of Mindset

"What you believe with certainty about money manifests in your reality."

Just like the *Wealth Building Formula (McT)*™ my *Six Steps to Wealth* can be used by the new or the experienced investor. For new people wanting to build wealth, it provides you with a step-by-step process. I go into great depth and detail about the Six Steps in my previous book, *You're Already a Wealth Heiress.*

I developed the *Six Steps to Wealth* to create a process that shows how to build wealth from scratch, because I saw a gap in what some financial experts were teaching. I believe financial experts get caught in the minutia of trying to save a dollar here and there, budgeting, improving your FICO score, or telling you how to get rid of debt. Those are good things to do, but ultimately, they won't change your life and move you from the lower middle class or middle class to upper class, or the top 1%. The only way to make a leap and close the wealth gap is by investing. That is getting your money working harder for you, so you don't have to work so hard.

To review again and for easy reference, the *Six Steps to Wealth* are:

1. Create a Wealthy Mindset
2. Save a Nest Egg
3. Find a Mentor
4. Invest in a Money Engine
5. Compound at a High Rate
6. Protect Your Wealth

Now that you are aware of superb money engines like cryptocurrencies, I truly believe the *Six Steps to Wealth* can be shortened into the *Three Steps to Quantum Wealth*. If you can turbo-charge your investment returns into a very high rate of compounding, now you are talking about making a quantum leap. Because of that, we can combine some of the steps and save time in getting you to financial freedom. This is truly life-changing. But I consider the most important first step is getting your thinking right, even before you start investing.

The Very Important First Step

When I developed the *Six Steps to Wealth,* I knew the first step had to be Create a Wealthy Mindset, and I am keeping that as the first Quantum Step. In my own wealth building journey as well as mentoring thousands of people, this step is crucial to laying the foundational belief system. It will determine your success or failure with money.

What does creating a wealthy mindset actually mean? Most people say, "Sure, I have a wealthy mindset." Yet, they don't realize that it is usually the single biggest factor about how successful they are or aren't. What they don't see is they have been subjected to some pretty intense impressions about money from their family and friends, life experiences, television, news and movies, and even some religious beliefs.

Here is the reality. People are conditioned to fear having wealth and fear losing wealth. In movies, TV shows and the news, we see countless negative interactions with money from the greedy tycoons to robbers, spendthrifts, celebrities and even homeless people, which encourages us to spend it, hoard it, think it is a burden and even get rid of it. All of these emotions are connected to money, and we have repeatedly been shown many of them. Rarely are we exposed to a role model with investing principles that are a good example and will create multi-generational wealth — not in school, not in movies, not on the news and often not even in our families.

As kids, we get strong messages about money that can stay with us. I remember when I was invited to go on a swim team trip to Florida for three days. It involved a flight from Seattle; two nights at a hotel; and money for meals, transfers and miscellaneous things that came to almost $1,500. My mom wouldn't let me go because she thought it was too expensive for a short trip. I was devastated because it seemed like everyone else was going. As a teenager, it was embarrassing. At 16, it was hard to understand the decisions parents make, especially when you are the youngest of five kids. Of course, I didn't consider the reason was my parents were paying for three college educations at once for my older siblings. As an adult, now I totally understand, but at the time, all I knew was the rest of the team was going and I wasn't. That experience internalized and in my distant memory, may make me feel pain around not doing or having things other people do, yet I may not consciously know why I feel that way.

As a child, you also hear strong beliefs about money at home. "Money doesn't grow on trees" or "What do you think I am, a money machine?" or "Do I look like an ATM?" or "We're not made of money." Our parents mean well, they are trying to teach us the value of money, but those statements don't explain what money is, or how to get it, or when it is ok to spend. As children we can become very confused and just feel bad bringing up the subject at all.

Parents' words can be a little brutal, depending on their financial situation. At home, we learn how to imitate our parents, so we end up taking on their habits and beliefs. As an adult, I understand the situation intellectually, but my emotional memory as a child will always be deep in my subconscious, unless replaced with new beliefs. I will share more about how to do that later.

Making Your First Million

We have also heard that "The first million dollars is the hardest to make." I agree with that, but the reason may surprise you. I believe the first million is the hardest to make because *you don't believe you can make it until you do*. Once you do, then you realize you can, so you do it again. That is what happened to me.

As I was investing in Internet stocks in 1998, my husband was very skeptical. He didn't believe my IRA account was going to pass $1 million. I believed it would because I was following the compounding rates of the stocks I invested in and knew it was only a matter of time before it would happen. This was during a bubble, and stock prices were escalating rapidly. I started keeping a running total for him on a piece of paper so I could update him. Since I had done a lot of work on creating my wealthy mindset, I was in good stead to achieve it. He kept being negative until one day, there it was in my investment account. He was shocked. From there, the money doubled in one year.

Maybe you already have a million dollars or more. If so, good work. If not, your own beliefs might be more along the lines of my late husband 20 years ago; he wanted a million dollars but didn't believe it was possible. You might think it feels like a fantasy: "Sure, I'd like a million dollars, who wouldn't?" Or perhaps "Maybe I'll win the lottery" is in your repertoire of thoughts. It's a nice dream, but simply not realistic. It's something you wouldn't refuse, but you don't realistically see it happening for you. Perhaps you even believe that if it did happen, it would be attached to something bad: "Wealth is such a burden. More wealth, more problems." I've heard that one a lot, and let me assure you, it is not true.

I've heard all kinds of weird theories about the bad things money brings, like "You will lose all of your friends" or "Everyone will ask you for money, and you will have to change your phone number." Yes, I've heard it all. None of it is true, in my opinion and experience.

Sure, if you act like a moron and tell everyone you are rich, then, of course, you can expect some consequences. But if you keep it to yourself, you will only find it makes life easier and more enjoyable. You can give to others, hire people to do work you don't want to do and throw fabulous parties. You can fund college for the grandkids, take a wonderful trip and buy some nice things. There is nothing "bad" about having more money. I have only found good things come from wealth, but I have also been responsible with it and not foolish or a showoff.

Removing Blocks and Embracing Certainty

Convincing yourself is the biggest block to your own wealth. On my podcast and in the *Wealth Heiress* book, I have shared how to remove blocks with specific instructions about wealth affirmations. Affirmations are repeating statements to remove blocks and create new beliefs as you want them to be. Once you start creating new beliefs, you are on your way to removing the blocks and replacing the limiting beliefs you have about money. Maybe you are asking if it is really that simple. Yes, it is. Our minds are much more powerful than we have been told.

I want to share with you the science behind mindset and money. That's right: Mindset and quantum mechanics play a role in your beliefs about wealth and whether you are using your thoughts to your advantage. Have you heard of the "Double Slit Experiment"? The Double Slit experiment proved how powerful our minds are at manifesting our beliefs. It was an experiment done decades ago and still isn't well understood by people. Let me explain.

Scientists wanted to find out if light was a wave or a particle, so they set up an experiment. It involved a piece of paper with two vertical slits in it and a movie screen behind it. In front of the paper, they pulsed photons (particles of light), so the particles moved through the slits. Because there were two vertical slits, they expected to see two vertical lines on the movie screen. And that is exactly what they saw.

Then they ran the experiment without observing the photons going through the slits. In other words, they ran the same experiment without watching or expecting results. What happened was astonishing. This time, instead of lining up in two vertical lines mimicking the slits, there was a wave pattern of photons across the movie screen. What on earth happened?

In the first experiment, the *belief and expectation* that the photons would mimic the slits caused them to mimic the slits. The observers were so certain of what would happen, that *they caused it to happen.* In the second experiment, when no one had an expectation and the light could pass through the slits without an observer, there was a wave of pure potential.

Certainty of thought is what creates the photons (and by the way, humans are made of photons of light) to behave to our expectation. In other words, *what you believe with certainty happens.* Our mind is so powerful, we actually impact our reality with what we believe will happen. What we believe with certainty is what we are likely to experience. It is very important you believe you can attain wealth and financial freedom in order for you to do so.

That is what I meant when I talked about being flippant about becoming a millionaire. Most people would like to be a millionaire, but they don't really believe they can become one. Like my beloved late husband, they are skeptical or even negative in their beliefs.

You need to create certainty in your beliefs so you can *use your belief to cause it to happen.* Belief at a subconsciuos level is important so you are congruent both in your conscious mind and in your subconscious. I will show you how to do that in a minute.

Think this mindset/belief/certainty turning into reality is far-fetched? Ah, then you must listen to how one woman's thoughts manifested millions. It is Cynthia Stafford's story.[26]

Tragically, one day Cynthia's brother was killed by a drunk driver, leaving behind five children. As their aunt, she saw the importance and urgency of being able to have enough money to quit her job and be a stay-at-home mom to the kids. Cynthia had been reading about the power of manifesting and wrote down an unusual number: $112 million — she made it a unique number (rather than a round $100 million) on purpose so it would be a sign to herself that she was the one who made it happen, if it did. The idea was if she could believe, really believe without doubt that she already had the money, the belief would cause the money

---

[26] Cynthia Stafford's $120 million Lottery Win, 9/10/14,
https://www.itwasonmyvisionboard.com/blog/cynthia-staffords-112-million-dollar-lottery-win

to appear. She began visualizing the money several times a day and used repetition of affirmations (the same principle I use in my teaching) to strengthen her beliefs. She slept with the piece of paper with $112 million written on it under her pillow and looked at it many times a day. It took about four months for her to really believe she had the money.

Repetition actually changes your beliefs by having you hear or see something so many times that you believe it to be true. It is like adding a piece of string every time you repeat something, until your belief is as thick as a rope. Why do you think advertisers on TV pay millions of dollars to repeat the same ads over and over? Repetition is how advertising works and *repetition changes and implants new beliefs in your subconscious.*

Repetition strengthened Cynthia's belief until she felt certain she already had $112 million. Soon after, she heard about a lottery with a prize of $112 million. Instantly, she felt certain it was the money she had attracted and believed she already had. She went to the store and bought one lottery ticket. Just one. Guess what happened? She had indeed won $112 million. It was on Mother's Day in 2007 and she quit her job to raise the children.

It took four months to create the certainty, but once she had it, the money appeared. *When she reached certainty with her desire, she was able to manifest it into reality.* Your wealthy mindset is much more powerful than you have been led to believe! While my expertise is not showing you how to manifest money out of thin air, the reason I'm telling you this is because I want to show you the power of absolute belief. You get what you believe you will get. I also want to make the point that repetition is a powerful way to change our beliefs and stop repelling wealth for unconscious reasons. So while my process is not about you manifesting the wealth through your beliefs, it is about changing any underlying, negative thoughts deep in your subconscious that might be holding you back from financial success.

An unfortunate side note: Because Cynthia gave a lot of her winnings away and invested in unsuccessful movie productions, the money was all gone in a few years. That is a sad and common story for new millionaires, unfortunately. We will talk about how to keep your wealth later, so you won't be like 70% of sudden millionaires who lose all of their money within five years.

Okay, maybe you are thinking that was a fluke. One person creating one outcome is not exactly a great experiment. For a real experiment, you need a control group and a placebo group. All experiments use a placebo group. Why is that? Because a placebo group shows results from doing nothing at all and *people are cured by just believing they have a cure.* The existence of placebo groups proves that belief can manifest an outcome. It happens all the time, even though we may not understand all of the reasons why.

Another example of the power of belief was a study done on people who had knee surgery. There were two groups: people who had knee surgery and knew it, and people who thought they had knee surgery, but didn't and were not told they didn't. For the second group, the experimenters opened up the knee with a scalpel, talked over the procedure as if they were doing it and sewed up the incision. However, they did not actually repair the knee. *About 45% of the people who thought they had knee surgery recovered as well as the people who had something done to their knees.*[27] Nothing had changed; it was the power of belief that caused the cure. They believed their problem was fixed and experienced no more pain.

And again, *"A new research study suggests that just thinking of exercising can have the same effects as actually hitting the gym, officials say."*[28] Indeed, what the mind believes is very powerful.

Repetition and Affirmations

Believing with certainty is the most powerful mindset there is. It's why a 110-pound woman can lift a car off her baby to save its life. She is *certain* she is going to save her baby. Your

[27] The BMJ, Use of Placebo Controls in the Evaluation of Surgery: Systematic Review, 5/21/14, https://www.bmj.com/content/348/bmj.g3253
[28] *Journal of Neurophysiology,* 12/25/14.

fears also come true when you are certain. "I just knew that was going to happen" is a form of certainty. "I knew I was going to marry him the moment I saw him. I knew I was going to get into an accident. I knew they were going to draw my number ..." And on it goes.

When you have certainty, you are imagining the event and causing the photons, or perhaps the vibration, to line up, so it happens. That is why creating a wealthy mindset is the first step to wealth and why the second million dollars is much easier to make than the first.

Get it? *How much wealth you have or don't have is directly related to what you believe with certainty.* If you want to improve your situation, get your mind certain. You do that with repetition of affirmative statements and using already-true sentences in between, just like I will show you.

I would like to quickly review here how to embrace certainty and new beliefs through repetition. These techniques work. That is why advertisers show commercials over and over. It is why you can still sing their jingles years later. Pop-pop, fizz-fizz; you know how it ends. With repetition of words, you can change your beliefs by substituting them for new ones: beliefs that will be positive for you and will align your photons into certainty so you can achieve what you want to.

Professional athletes have used affirmations for years. Muhammad Ali once said, *"I am the greatest. I said that even before I knew I was."*[29] This is one of my favorite quotes from Ali. It's very honest, because he is admitting he used affirmations until he believed in himself and his abilities with certainty.

The way I recommend you use affirmations is a little different, because what I found is that our subconscious will argue with us if we consciously try to change our beliefs. When you read a positive statement that you don't believe to be true, you will get pushback in the form of internal dialogue with your subconscious. That is why traditional affirmations don't work well. What happens is this: You read the affirmation "I'm worth

---

[29] *BrainyQuote.com website.*

$20 million." Your subconscious says, "No, you're not. That is not true." Your conscious mind reads it again, and you get the same argument.

Here is how you stop that from happening. You put "already true" statements in between each sentence, so that by the time your subconscious tries to push back and say it is not true, you have moved on to the true statement it will agree with. It looks like this: *I'm worth $20 million. My name is Linda (already true statement; insert your name in place of mine).* This allows your subconscious to accept the belief instead of arguing with you, and it allows the belief to sink into your subconscious. Repeat this over and over.

Vision boards also help strengthen your beliefs, because you are looking at them frequently and the repetition is reinforcing your belief. Wealth journals and written goals help for the same reason. They are all tools, but visualizing in your mind — seeing and hearing your goal accomplished — is how you are going to strengthen your beliefs. We know with visualization your mind can't tell the difference between what is real and what is imagined. You get what you believe, so start molding your belief system into certainty *immediately*!

One thing that I have found to be true is to listen to my inner voice and pay attention to questions that come up. If my mind wants to know something, I seek out the answer, which has often led me to the exact piece of information I needed to move forward or to make a leap. Your inner voice is the best guide to listen to for advancing your wealth-building. Listen to it and pay attention to your gut feelings.

Overcoming Blocks and Limiting Beliefs

Earlier in this chapter, I talked about how your beliefs about money are shaped by society and people who influence you. How can you overcome some of the more common beliefs that will stop you from attaining wealth and financial freedom in the quantum age? Let's talk about some of the common blocks and limiting beliefs I hear from people.

"Mo' money, mo' problems." I've seen this tweeted or written on Facebook. If your mindset is that more money equals more problems, then you believe that more money is bad. If you believe more money is bad, what do you think your subconscious will be directing you to do every time you have the opportunity for more money? It will probably choose to get rid of it, pass on receiving it, spend it — anything but keeping more of it. This is an awful belief system that is destined for disaster. If you believe this or have ever written this, change your limiting beliefs and replace it with a positive money belief using my affirmation strategy.

Having more money is a good thing. It allows you to have more freedom, and who doesn't want that? If you want to help others, you can afford it. If you don't want to paint your house, you can pay someone to do it. If you want to see the world, you can afford whatever means of transportation you want to take. If you are ever stranded somewhere, you can afford to pay someone to rescue you. If you have a serious health problem, you can afford the best health care. There is nothing inherently bad about having more money!

Just realize that if you are not knowledgeable about money, the answer to the problem isn't more money. If you are "bad" with money, more money is *not* the solution, because more money just means you will make the same bad decisions with more money until you don't have any. The solution is to *know what to do with money*, so you can make it work harder for you and you don't have to work so hard.

"If I ever get a lot of money, I'll just lose it." If you are fearful of money, it will be something you repel. Some people are afraid of what to do with money if they have a lot of it. Before they even have a lot of money, they are setting themselves up for failure. If that is the case, what are your chances of being successful with money? What are the chances you will manage it well? If you have money problems now, having more money is not the answer because you will do the same things over and over, and make the same mistakes. If you have problems with having enough money, it is probably because you don't have good habits, you have faulty beliefs about money or you are not aware of what the best choices are for your money.

"I won't believe it until I see the check in the bank." Remember when I talked about the Double Slit experiment? We learned that your thoughts direct the photons to line up in the way you expect. You get what your thoughts believe. Yet there is a hesitation to be positive and sometimes people decide to be doubtful and believe only after something happens. When you have that attitude, it is fighting with your power to have a positive expectation that you make happen. You are telling the universe, "I don't have this power and I don't believe." You are making yourself work harder for it to happen. This is not a wealth mindset. What you want to do is visualize the check in the bank, believe it will happen and help the photons line up for the outcome you desire. Positive expectation is more powerful than being a skeptic. That is having a wealthy mindset.

"I could kick myself for not investing." There is no room for perfection when investing. Sometimes people are obsessed with buying at the absolute bottom during a dip, when even great investors have a hard time doing that. Yes, you can look at all the technical analysis and try to predict the low, but the reality is that as an investor, I am less concerned with how much I acquired the asset for and more concerned that I own the right asset. In other words, it is more important that you own cryptocurrency than the price you paid for it.

There is No Perfection in Investing

People who never bought cryptocurrency missed out on spectacular returns. People who invested in cryptocurrency like XRP, Ethereum and bitcoin turned $1,000 into six figures in five years. Did it matter if they paid $0.10 or $0.25 for each crypto? Not in the grand scheme of things. Don't worry about being perfect or paying the absolute lowest price. You will be happy with your investments anyway. It is better to own the asset at a higher price than to wait for a cheaper price and never buy, which happens to many people. Then they kick themselves for not buying for years to come.

It is not what you invest in that you regret; it is what you didn't invest in that you regret. As one venture capitalist said, what keeps him awake at night are not the companies he invested in but the companies he said "no" to that went on to be worth billions of dollars.

You can't go back in time and change things, so it's best not to think "coulda, woulda, shoulda." What purpose does that serve but frustration? There is absolutely nothing you can do about it except learn from your mistakes and do better next time. There are always opportunities to make a lot of money; there is no shortage. To think you missed "the one" is simply not accurate.

We are always moving through cycles, and assets are moving from low to high and high to low over time. Once you understand that, you will know how to look for opportunities. For example, if you understand that we just finished an almost-perfect 40-year interest rate cycle, then you will understand that for the next 40 years, interest rates are likely to rise and approximately 40 years from now will be the peak. That will be a headwind for real estate, bonds and financial instruments, and a boon for physical assets like commodities, land, farms, precious metals, art, rare earths, gemstones, etc.

Of course, I believe cryptocurrencies will do the best of all. There are assets to be had cheaply today that are bottoming in this cycle and will do well for the next 40 years. With cryptocurrencies, the time needed to compound and build wealth has been reduced by many years. If you understand how cycles work, they will help you invest and identify areas of growth for decades.

Shift Your Thinking

I have found their subconscious thoughts and beliefs about wealth are much more important than knowledge about great investments. We have been taught so many things by our families, teachers, bosses and the school of hard knocks. But how much really serves us? Is it accurate? What beliefs do people who have wealth have that maybe you don't? Is it important?

Yes, your subconscious is very important. It is one of the reasons we have such a divide between the rich and the poor today. Never before in history have we seen such a wealth gap between the haves and have nots. I believe that is because of education. Not as in college, although it is true that people who go to college earn more money than people who don't. I'm talking about education about money, mindset and how to invest.

I was fortunate to grow up in a household that taught me money must be invested for it to grow. My parents had five children, and I'm the youngest. Mom stayed at home with us, and Dad earned a modest salary as an engineer at Boeing. Mom managed our family's real estate investments and understood that money had to be invested to grow. As a homemaker, she was extremely busy, but she still managed to locate real estate investments for our family. Her dad was a builder, so perhaps she learned from her parents' experience of investing.

That is where I believe the divide happens: You either learn to invest and grow your money or you don't. If you don't learn that it is important, you won't make investments that compound your money. You won't understand the importance of investing in a 401(k). You won't take the time to learn about investments. You might not even invest in a home (and now the prices are so high that home ownership is out of reach for many). But with that one belief about investing money so it grows and compounds, you may end up at the end of your life with millions of dollars made from your investments.

Change Your Mindset, Change Your Money

Changing your mindset to make your money work hard for you is the most important decision you can make about your finances. Quite simply, most people don't get wealthy because of a salary; they get wealthy because of a business or investments, which have the potential to compound at a high rate. This book is giving you the road map, so you benefit from the most exciting investment opportunities in generations. High compounding rates also mean that money will come to you sooner, which I am sure you won't be sad about.

We will talk more about cycles and how they can help us navigate investing. It is the most underrated and important investing tool there is, and I can't wait to share it with you. The Internet brought us a technology cycle that we hadn't seen in our lifetimes, and it is about to repeat — and be bigger this time. But before we get into investing and compounding money, we have to overcome fear.

Fear Doesn't Serve You

One of the biggest obstacles people have in creating a wealthy mindset is they are dealing with constant fear. Fear comes from watching television and hearing bad news all of the time, which is a negative form of repetition. If they invest, people fear they will lose all of their money. They fear fluctuation of the value of their cryptos or stocks. Being scared is OK, but don't make investing decisions because of fear. When feeling fear, the best way to get out of that mindset is to list things you are grateful for. The antidote to fear is gratitude.

Fear and gratitude cannot exist in your mind at the same time. If you want to get unstuck and out of fear-based beliefs, the way is through gratitude. When you are grateful for what you have, you attract more of it. When you are grateful, you are in an optimistic mood. When you are fearful, you are in a pessimistic mood. Optimism wins every time because certainty is what is directing your energy forward to make success happen. When you have certainty, your photons are aligning with your vision. If you want to create a wealthy mindset and get out of fear, stay in gratitude.

If you don't know how to feel more grateful, I recommend you write down 100 things you are grateful for. They can be anything at all; it doesn't really matter. What you will soon understand is your focus will shift from fear to gratitude and you realize you feel grateful for everything. It works.

The Next Step

The next step in the *Six Steps to Wealth* would normally be to save a nest egg. Unfortunately, many people don't save much of a nest egg, and may not have that much money to invest. That keeps people from leaping above their financial status and achieving their financial goals. The people who have the greatest chance of building wealth then become the business owners, because their businesses grow and become worth a lot. Otherwise, lack of a nest egg has presented a problem for many people in achieving their goal of financial freedom.

Not anymore. Because of the high compounding rates of cryptocurrencies, you no longer need a large nest egg to invest. Even small amounts of money can grow into crazy wealth because you are investing very early and during a technological revolution. What would normally take decades for you to save money and create a nest egg to invest can be leaped over. Therefore, we can skip this step and go right to Step 2 to Quantum Wealth: Find a Mentor.

The Bottom Line

Your mind is powerful, and your mindset is the foundation of achieving wealth. There are very specific strategies to use to change your mindset from non-belief to believing. What you believe with certainty will come to pass.

Leap into the Quantum Age

Answer these questions:

- What do you believe about money and wealth?
- Are you aware of any money blocks you have?
- What did you learn about money from growing up in your family?
- What does being rich or wealthy mean to you?
- What do you need to be rich? How much money do you need to be rich?
- Do you believe it is possible for you to become rich? Why or why not?
- What is stopping you from having what you want?

- What small step forward can you take to get going in the right direction?

- What affirmations do you want to repeat and believe? Write them down.

Chapter 12
Step Two to Quantum Wealth: Find a Mentor

"Working with a mentor means you can shorten the path to your destination."

Fidelity Investments did a study of millionaires and found many had traits in common:

1. They set ambitious goals and act on them.
2. **They have mentors.**
3. They look for feedback.
4. They are not afraid of failure.
5. They understand the value of time.

Of course, these steps are self-explanatory, but I want to point out that the study said, *"Many self-made millionaires are quick to admit that they cannot possibly know how to do everything. They reach out to others who know the ins and outs of different types of saving and investing, tapping into the best minds on each subject for perspective and insight. That certainly pays off."*[30]

Having a mentor is a proven trait among existing millionaires. A mentor is someone who can guide you in the right direction based on their experience and save you time reaching your destination.

Find a Mentor Who Matches Your Desired Lifestyle

It is important that your mentor's advice matches your desired lifestyle. For example, I couldn't relate to the frugalist movement where people are encouraged to be misers, not go out

[30] Stella Morrison, *Business News Daily*, 7/29/21, https://www.businessnewsdaily.com/2871-how-most-millionaires-got-rich.html

to eat or drink, live a meager life, and try to save every penny they can, investing some of the money saved in the stock market. I agreed with the investing in the stock market part, but I couldn't agree with scrimping for every cent. To me, life is meant to be abundant and there are so many incredible places to travel to, restaurants to taste fantastic food and new people to meet.

It seems like frugalists are putting money ahead of living, and I can't condone that. I believe you can make enough money to live well and have a full life, even if you don't have a high income. There is no need to live a meager existence or soon you will be living in a tent in the woods. Following the Financial Independence Retire Early (FIRE) movement was not for me.

Yes, retiring early can be great. I did it myself, but I became terribly bored. We all need challenges and growth, so it is up to you how you arrange your life to get it. For myself, I believe in buying quality items on sale, enjoying some luxuries, living life to the fullest and giving back to humanity.

It is a problem if your mentor does not share the same view of life as you do. If they believe you need to budget every penny and you don't like that approach, move on. I could never follow the stingy financial experts who restrict spending. I have never found that to be the key to wealth.

Questions to See if You and Your Mentor are a Match

Check in with yourself and make sure you feel good about what you are learning and the steps you are taking with your mentor. Here are a few things you want to look for in a mentor and questions to ask yourself:

- Has the mentor done what you want to accomplish?
- Do you resonate with their style and what they are teaching?
- Do you feel better after learning from them?
- Is your mind expanding with new concepts?
- Are you learning new things you have not heard before?

- Are they respectful to others and not haughty or belittling?

- Are they helping you move in the direction you want to go financially?

- Is the lifestyle they project the one you would like to have?

It doesn't mean you have to search far and wide for a wise soul, but you do want to find someone who can show you the way.

Check Your Mentor's Mindset

I have told you how important mindset is and that I believe it is foundational to wealth-building. Early in my life, I was introduced to books like *Think and Grow Rich* by Napoleon Hill. I loved the concept of positive thinking and that our minds are much more powerful in manifestation than we give them — or ourselves — credit for. This led me to books like *The Magic of Believing*, *The Magic of Thinking Big*, *As a Man Thinketh* and more. Later I read books like *How to Make Money in Stocks* by William J. O'Neil to learn how to invest in stocks.

In my family life, my mother and father were incredible role models and mentors because they were real estate investors. They owned an apartment building, and my brothers and sisters and I earned our allowances by working at the building, whether it was painting, vacuuming, washing windows, cleaning, etc. We worked to earn money. That gave us great skills and also gave us first-hand experience in what it was like to be a property owner.

Mom raised five children while managing our investments, dealing with renters and leases, etc., so we saw first-hand how a businesswoman can operate from home and be a successful investor. She was very conscious about how to minimize taxes, so we even learned there were investments that can help lower taxes. We absorbed a lot, and I'm proud to say we all have had financial success, which I trace back to Mom and Dad as mentors. We were lucky to have great role models and mentors in our parents.

But even if your parents aren't or weren't great mentors, it is easier than ever to find a mentor because of the Internet. There are podcasts, videos and websites, in addition to books, to help you learn anything you want to know. Everyone has the ability to be financially savvy with the amount of free financial information at our fingertips. Any answer to your question is a quick search away. Just make sure it is from a trusted source.

Financial Advisors are Not Mentors

It is hard to have a financial advisor as your mentor, because their business model is not to teach you. Their business model is to gather assets, so as soon as you have invested with them, they are off finding more assets to invest from someone else.

There is nothing wrong with that; it is just that Wall Street is not set up to educate you. In fact, Wall Streeters are good at complicating things to convince you it is too complex for you to invest on your own. Using jargon that seems like a foreign language, sending you charts and graphs, and talking a lot about economics is a way to turn you off from even asking questions.

Rather, you want to find a mentor who makes investing understandable, can explain it in plain English and seems to know what you need to know next before you even ask. A good mentor points out what is important among the economic data points to show you the most important one or two you need to pay attention to. They clear away all the dust and debris of excess data, so you understand what is happening and why. Sometimes they introduce you to something you didn't know before, like cycles, and show you where they are effective.

They teach you things that they learned from experience. Follow someone who has accomplished what you want to accomplish, so they can show you the direct route. The important thing is that they have done it. Lots of people want to tell you how they *think* you can become a millionaire, but it is apparent they do not really know. They just *think* they know.

In the Quantum Age, things are happening at light speed. The financial landscape is constantly changing because of all the disruptive technology. You must have a mentor who is on top of this on a daily basis. Throughout this book, I have given you very concrete recommendations with the strong caveat that they are given at a certain moment in time and will be evolving as technology evolves. I have used them primarily as examples of how my analysis works.

What my *Be Wealthy & Smart VIP Experience* group knows is that I am with them on a daily, weekly and monthly basis. I am always available to answer questions. In a short weekly summary, they are informed up-to-the-minute about what is happening in financial markets, whether that is the stock market, precious metals or cryptocurrencies. That is why they have chosen me as their wealth mentor. It is not just about my good investment recommendations; it is about guidance about when to buy the dips and when to hold through volatility, and giving them the confidence to know what they own and why.

Work Closely with Your Mentor

If you have a chance to work closely with a mentor, it can get you where you want to go much faster. I have invested in mentors for business with great success. Mentors can keep you from making mistakes and help you leap ahead. Once you find a financial expert whom you relate to and whose style you like, it is a matter of learning all you can from them. If they have a paid program, consider joining. There is no better investment than investing in yourself and your knowledge. Just take a look at Taylor.

Taylor was letting the volatility of cryptocurrencies rattle her emotions. She was always panicking and selling at the bottom, only to regret it later. After joining my VIP group, she was kept informed about what the charts were saying the next direction would be, which helped her buy the dips, kept her focused on the long term and inspired her to stay confident in her investments regardless of volatility. She ended up making six figures in her crypto portfolio from a small initial investment and was thrilled to have conquered her fear.

The Bottom Line

Mentors come to you in many ways. Direct interaction with an individual you trust, books and podcasts are all powerful mentoring tools. They are essential to helping you get to the heart of the matter and map out your financial wealth strategy.

Leap into the Quantum Age

1. Look at the gaps you have in knowledge you need and find a mentor in each area, whether it is from a book, podcast or other source.

2. Write down who is on your financial team. Who do you have, and who are you missing?

3. Take a hard look at your financial team. Are they reaching out to you proactively or must you call them? Are they keeping your informed about your money and markets in an easy-to-understand way? Do you feel well-informed about your investments? Are they helping you continuously increase your financial knowledge? Are you getting what you need or are you settling for less? If the latter, why?

Chapter 13

Step 3 to Quantum Wealth: Invest in a Money Engine and Compound at a High Rate

"Compounding at a high rate has never been easier than by investing in cryptocurrencies."

In Step 3 to Quantum Wealth, I have combined another two of the *Six Steps to Wealth* into one. What were previously Step 4: Investing in a Money Engine, and Step 5: Compounding at a High Rate, are accomplished by investing in cryptocurrencies. The high rates of compounding that I have shared with you are the real differentiators. As I have shown, they will literally shave years off of the time it takes you to accumulate wealth and attain financial freedom. We will focus on them in this chapter and talk about Step 6 to Wealth, Protecting Your Wealth, in a later chapter.

Invest in a Money Engine

A money engine is simply an investment (stocks, bonds, ETFs, precious metals, real estate, businesses, etc.) that grows your wealth and will take you to your desired financial destination. Think of it in terms of travel. If you want to get from Los Angeles to New York City, you usually take a plane. The speed with which you arrive depends on the vehicle you choose and how fast it is traveling. Investments are the same way.

You can invest in stocks, mutual funds, Exchange Traded Funds (ETFs — a basket of stocks that represent a stock index), cryptocurrencies or real estate. One way might be faster than another in terms of compounding rate, depending on the cycle and other factors. There is no one right road, just like there is no one perfect type of transportation. It depends on what you are trying to accomplish. Some transportation is faster than others, and that is the same as with money engines.

Although I have mentioned individual stocks a lot, they are not the easiest or most practical investment. I highly recommend you invest using ETFs instead of mutual funds because they have low expenses and mirror the index's performance. For example, the S & P 500 is an index of the largest 500 companies in the U.S. You can buy all 500 in one ETF. ETFs have gained popularity because they have outperformed actively managed mutual funds and are less expensive. Today, you have a wide variety of ETFs to choose from.

Sadly, money managers of mutual funds have not outperformed index averages for years. If they aren't getting you better returns, then they don't deserve to earn the additional fees you have to pay them. Why pay extra fees to a money manager who is not outperforming the index averages?

I have mentioned the importance of asset allocation and investing in different asset classes in your 401(k). In addition to the usual asset classes of large cap, mid-cap, small cap, international, emerging markets and short-term bonds, you can add industry-specific funds like real estate investment trusts (REITs), specific countries like India or sectors like precious metals. If you want to own retail stores, you could buy an ETF that is a basket of retail stores. It just makes investing easier. Sector ETFs such as technology, precious metals, commodities and real estate are invested in one industry, so they are considered non-diversified ETFs. All of the companies in the ETF will tend to move higher or lower together since they are in the same business sector.

There will be ups and downs when investing in the stock market, but, in my mind, using ETFs is the right way to go for a long-term investor. It is going to get you to the higher rates of compounding that we have talked a lot about, without requiring a lot of effort, time or trouble on your part. Whether you are a beginner or an investing pro, ETFs make a lot of sense and belong in your portfolio.

The exception is crypto ETFs. I do not recommend investing in crypto ETFs. The fees are very high (2.5% annually), and they are not properly diversified. For example, 80% of their assets are in one cryptocurrency — bitcoin. You are much better off creating your own portfolio of cryptocurrencies and investing in them directly, rather than paying huge fees for someone else to do it for you. I think you would be smarter to create your own ETF and buy the cryptos I have recommended. You would pay fees to purchase the cryptos but would have no ongoing fees if you bought them directly yourself. In my opinion, a crypto ETF should have about 30 coins and be more evenly weighted among cryptos.

Cryptocurrencies as an Asset Class

Cryptocurrencies are one of the most undervalued asset classes, compared to many other money engines. Cryptocurrencies are in their infancy and, as I have shared with you many times in this book, an early-stage company's compounding rates can be explosive for years. This is a unique time to invest, when you can get into a thriving, fast-growing asset class such as cryptocurrency ahead of the crowd.

Investing in cryptocurrencies can *save you decades of time,* more than if you had invested in stocks. You have already learned that bitcoin is the fastest-growing asset to reach $1 trillion of value in history. You now know other cryptocurrencies are now growing even faster than bitcoin. Digital assets are more like early-stage investments and are a different asset class from stocks. They will act differently. Digital assets will grow faster, be more volatile and correct harder. The pullbacks in price can be dramatic, but so is the upside. As long as it is still in a strong upward trend, AKA bull market, don't let the pullbacks worry you.

For the baby boomer, this means early retirement or a fuller life in retirement. For the GenXer or millennial, it might mean early retirement, an improved lifestyle allowing you to travel more, and having a nicer car and home. Maybe even multiple homes. Pay for multiple college educations for your children or grandchildren. It also will give you funds to be more charitable and help others. The potential is up to you.

Let's compare rates of return of different investments for 10 years, with assets you are familiar with, and see what happened.

Traditional Methods of Compounding vs. Cryptocurrencies

If you invested in gold over the last 10 years, your compounding rate would have been 1.72%. If you invested in long-dated U.S. Treasuries, your compounding rate would have been 4.58% annually. If you invested in the S & P 500, your compounding rate would have been 11.22%. If you invested in the NASDAQ (tech stock index), your rate of compounding would have been 16.94% annually. If you invested in Amazon, your compounding rate would have been 33.5% annually. If you invested in Tesla, your compounding rate would have been 63.8% annually. If you invested in bitcoin, your compounding rate would have been 196.72%. Remember, bitcoin got a head start because it was the first cryptocurrency, but other cryptocurrencies are surpassing its performance, as you will see.

Compound at a High Rate

I used to say that the more time that you have in regard to compounding money or the higher the rate that you can compound at consistently, the faster you are going to build wealth, but now, because cryptocurrencies are compounding at such high rates, you don't need as much time to compound.

You have learned that you can maximize your compounding rate by taking advantage of the right assets and cycles. If you have a high rate of compounding, it makes up for any lack of money you have to invest and saves you years of saving to invest. It also reduces the time it takes to grow your investment into millions of dollars, so your time of leaving your money in an investment to grow has also shortened. That is why I am so thrilled to hear that millennials have 25% of their investing funds in cryptocurrencies — because I know that it will grow faster for them, and they won't have to wait a lifetime to reap the rewards.

During times when interest rates are low, people can often get confused about the idea of compounding at a higher rate. I just want to say it is easy to get caught up in thinking small and believing there is no way to improve your situation. Nothing can be farther from the truth. You need to get outside of your comfort zone, and that is where most people get stuck. It might boggle your mind to see the kind of compounding rates I am showing you.

What is so incredible is that I am using real rates of return that have already happened with cryptocurrencies. This is not a "what if magic happened?" Rather, it is "this is what happened to early adopters in crypto." I am taking real numbers and looking backward. I can't promise these returns will continue in the future, but I have given you many reasons why they might.

Let's say you have saved a six-figure nest egg, have 20 years until retirement and know the right stocks to invest in. If the stock market performs better than its long-term average, here's what is possible: $100,000 × 20 years × 12 percent = $964,629 (close to $1 million). Well-done in traditional investing terms.

Now let's say you don't have a lump sum, but you can invest $10,000 a year into your company stock plan. If you got extraordinarily lucky and the stock grew at 100% per year, your $10,000 compounded at 100 percent would grow to $1 million in about seven years. You invested $10,000 per year for seven years or $70,000. Right there, you have shaved $30,000 off ($100,000 − $70,000) of what you needed to save in the prior example and 13 years off (20 years − 7 years) of the time it took to compound your money. That is what compounding at a high rate will do: reduce the time and money part of the equation so you need to invest less money and you will achieve your goals sooner.

But what if you only had $1,000 to invest? What could you possibly do to have that grow into a meaningful amount? Let's look at a stock example first. If you are able to compound at the typical return in the stock market, $1,000 × 5 years × 10 percent = $1,610. Now let's give you the benefit of the doubt and say you got lucky with your company stock again and compounded at 100% for five years; it would grow to $32,000. Great compounding rate, but not enough money to retire.

Now I am going to share with you *real returns* that happened over the last five years in the largest cryptocurrencies. If you invested $1,000 in bitcoin and Ethereum in 2016, here is what they would be worth in 2021:

| Bitcoin | $148,194 |
| Ethereum | $273,716 |

These are real returns. I know returns greater than 100 percent sound impossible. We are used to seeing 1 or 2% when we go to the bank. We are used to earning 10% in the stock market. But remember, this is a different asset class. It is not like anything else. Also, I have told you that small businesses often grow at 100 percent to thousands of percent per year, at least for the first several years. That is why small business owners become millionaires the most. It is because they get the higher compounding rates — they can get growth rates into the hundreds and thousands of percent. So can cryptocurrencies.

Please do not misunderstand me. I am not saying that a 100% rate of return is something that is a done deal going forward. No one can promise the future. I am simply making the point that when you look at compounding, you need to understand how cryptocurrency compounding works and that it is possible to get to compounding rates that can get you to $1 million.

This is not something that you will hear on the news. If you want to know where to invest and how to build wealth, a wealth mentor is whom you need to listen to. It is not a promise of what you will earn; it is potential for what you *might* earn. But many people will go through life working hard and won't know that investing could be their ticket to financial freedom. I want to make sure you know what compounding rates the technological revolution is bringing.

Let's keep on looking at the numbers. As we just discussed, in a normal year, we expect a return in the stock market of about 10%. That is the long-term average. However, for the past five years, the S & P 500 has averaged 14% per year. That's 40% above average. The higher compounding rates, the better.

Now let's compare what $1,000 invested into the best performing stocks and cryptocurrencies are over five years. First, let's look at what $1,000 invested in some of the best-performing stocks has grown to in five years:

Facebook	$2,803
Google	$3,016
Microsoft	$4,670
Apple	$4,799

Fantastic: In five years, you made almost five times your investment by investing in Apple.

Now let's see which stock investments performed even better. A $1,000 investment in these stocks for five years has grown to:

Netflix	$5,050
Amazon	$5,530
PayPal	$7,101
Tesla	$14,975
Nvidia	$17,071

Great! Your $1,000 investment multiplied *17 times* when invested in Nvidia.

Let's see what stock investments performed even better. Your $1,000 invested in these companies has grown to:

Etsy	$26,388
AMD	$28,639
Shopify	$41,662

Wow, a *41x return* on Shopify. These are excellent returns for stocks. It is amazing how money has compounded in some Wall Street favorites, *but* as you will see, it is nothing compared to cryptocurrency compounding returns!

Remember?

If you invested $1,000 for five years in these cryptocurrencies, each would be worth over two to twenty-four times as much as the best performing stock:

Litecoin	$87,900
XRP	$267,900
Dogecoin	$1,030,000

Yes: In five years $1,000 grew to $87,900 in Litecoin, $267,900 in XRP and $1,030,000 in Dogecoin. You literally earned decades of stock investment returns in a few years in the top cryptocurrencies. Even great-performing stocks like Shopify and Tesla have only done a fraction of what the cryptocurrencies have. *Do you see how you have reduced the time it takes to build wealth by at least a decade?*

I have a compounding calculator at https://LindaPJones.com that allows you to insert the current principal, years to grow and interest rate. It also lets you add money each year so you can see what you need to do in terms of additional funding to reach your goal faster.

Although these past returns are astounding, these are only three of eight dominant winning technologies which I have given you in this book.

Don't Invest by Looking in the Rear View Mirror

Here is another important piece of advice: Look ahead to determine what money engines deserve your investment. Most investors are trained to look backward at performance from the prior decade to choose their investments. That has nothing to do with the next decade. In fact, it is likely that the next decade's best performance will not come from the same place it did during the previous decade because it is already high.

For example, the bond market had a spectacular 40-year cycle. Interest rates peaked in 1980 at a 20% Fed Funds rate, which is the cost financial institutions charge each other for money. Once interest rates started coming down, bond interest rates also dropped. As interest rates decline, the value of a bond rises, so dropping interest rates provide gains on bonds.

What happens when the opposite occurs — when interest rates rise? Bond valuations decline. If you expected bonds to go up after interest rates started to rise, you would be mistaken. The value of a bond will not move the same way in a rising interest rate market as it did in a falling interest rate market, yet asset allocation models still suggest large percentages of long-term bonds in your portfolio as if they are "safe." They are not safe in a rising-interest-rate environment. It is impossible for bonds to have the gains they had in the last cycle when rates are at 2% today.

These are the kinds of things you want to be looking at when making investment decisions and choosing your money engines. You want to be aware of why something performed the way it did.

Where can you invest now to take advantage of these trends? Again, you want to look at where the market is likely to go, not where we have been. We have had cycles like gold going up very well in the 1970s, oil in the 1980s, stocks in the 1990s and real estate in the 2000s.

We are so early; we are invested even before the 1% richest are. The big wave of money will come into cryptocurrencies. It will make the compounding rates even higher. But when it is a bubble, everyone will be talking favorably about investing in them, which is far from the case today.

The next cycle is usually something that is under the radar and not everyone is talking about or seeing, just like cryptocurrencies today. We are years away from a peak, but someday, as they get closer to their peak, then the masses will begin to see, and the superior investment will become obvious. Then everyone jumps in, and it becomes a bubble peak. The bubble pops, and then we start all over again. More about this in the next chapter when we explore the 12 Signs of a Bubble.

Don't Use Leverage

As long as you continue to be smart with your money and not go on a spending rampage, I will show you how to make it last for a lifetime or even for generations with my Five Steps to Maintaining Your Wealth.

You need to protect your wealth legally with documents like wills, as well as eliminate leverage that you used to build wealth. You do not want to lose the wealth you just created. Once you have achieved wealth, it is important to pay off your debt and then diversify. If you do not and remain leveraged, that leverage can sink your net worth as fast as it built it if the asset depreciates or the market declines.

Let me give you an example. Michael borrowed money to buy real estate in Scottsdale. As soon as properties increased in value, he used them as collateral to buy more properties. Since home values kept rising, this cycle repeated over and over. Unfortunately, instead of being satisfied with creating millions and stopping at a reasonable point, Michael kept leveraging and never paid off the original debt, only to lose it all when the housing market crashed.

I have seen a lot of money made by leveraging and buying a strong-performing investment engine, only to be lost when that investment trend stops. Diversifying can help protect your wealth. It is a defensive measure, not an offensive measure. Millionaires know diversifying slows your wealth-building on the way up, but it also protects you from ruin in a declining market.

Don't use leverage to invest or speculate. I don't recommend trying to bet on the direction of the crypto market. This is a very high-risk strategy that can backfire. It is much wiser to carefully select which cryptocurrencies to invest in, then allocate 3% to 5% of your assets and hold for the long term.

When you are compounding, it is very important that you not withdraw any of the funds so you can let them compound. Once your money is compounding, leave it alone. If you have it in real estate as a long-term investment or if you have it in something that is going to be a long-term cycle, leave it in for the cycle. Give it time to grow, and typically you should allow it to continue to multiply.

Now let's turn to some important investing principles you need to know for financial freedom in the Quantum Age.

The Bottom Line

Step 3 to Quantum Wealth activates the power of money engines and your ability to compound at high rates with an eye to the future. The Quantum Age has changed many things, but compounding smartly is a core component no matter what.

Leap into the Quantum Age

Look at what the next business, interest rate and inflation cycles are likely to bring. If we are at zero interest rates, they can only go one direction in the future. If we are at low inflation, it is likely to go up. If we are in a recession, eventually it will recover. If the economy is booming, the next phase is likely to be a recession.

Instead of looking in the rearview mirror, here are some questions you need to be asking with the help of your mentors:

• Where are we in the economic cycle?

• What is changing a lot in price?

• What is the next cycle that is going to perform the best?

• Where are interest rates — are they at an extreme low or high?

159

Section Four

Staying Wealthy in the Quantum Age

"To live richer is to follow the inner path to wealth and abundance. This includes the progressive realization of worthy goals, to love and have compassion and, most importantly, to always be in touch with your creative consciousness, which is the source of all riches."

– Deepak Chopra

Chapter 14
Cycles Exist Even if You Don't Believe in Them

"Cycles exist in nature and the stock market. They are hidden knowledge that has been tightly guarded by some of the wealthiest and most powerful people who use it to their advantage."

I am going to discuss some heady stuff now. You might find it a bit much, but I want to tell you that this changed my whole view of investing. You might need to grab a cup of coffee or maybe a glass of wine before you begin. I will go into a lot of detail; you can read it once and then come back to it if you find that works best for you.

What I am going to explain is how cycles exist in both nature and the stock market. This is hidden knowledge that has been tightly guarded by some of the wealthiest and most powerful people, who use it to their advantage without sharing it with you. Yes, some of this is already known, but we are only going to touch the surface.

From my time working on Wall Street as a money manager and representing investments that competed against Goldman Sachs, I knew the firm to be one of the best at money management. Anyone who had helped them be at the top got my attention, such as Dr. Charles Nenner, who had been a market timer for Goldman Sachs.

One day in 2008, I heard Dr. Nenner during a TV interview make these comments:

> "*Markets do not move at random, and there is no way of influencing their behavior. Markets are part of creation and follow natural laws...However, once you understand the power of cycles, the correlation to market moves are uncanny. Patterns of past market actions and reactions*

repeat and are therefore predictable...Do things move at random or don't move at random? If they move at random, there's nothing you should read, because you don't know what happens tomorrow. If they don't move at random, then you have to look for the underlying systematic of what happens...Economic cycles are very long-term cycles, and they are very predictable. "[31]

His words really struck me, and I started subscribing to his research. What I learned was that cycles repeat at regular intervals, which make them able to predict future events. I learned that sometimes — but not always — they are so accurate they can predict an event to the exact day, years in advance. I also learned that cycles had been quietly used by successful and wealthy investors.

The Foundation for the Study of Cycles (FSC), which began when President Herbert Hoover hired Harvard economist Edward Dewey to investigate what caused the Great Depression, was one of the first to discover cycles. The organization has documented 4,200 cycles on the planet. Dewey was able to eliminate all the reasons you might think caused the Depression, such as layoffs and economic policy. After the 1929 crash and resulting depression, he found that cycles were more useful for predicting economic events than any amount of economic theory that he had learned. Cycles repeated and appeared in history at regular intervals.

Prominent entrepreneurs like George Westinghouse started backing Dewey's research. Other important businesspeople in 1931 heard about the project and formed a committee. Out of that committee, the Foundation for the Study of Cycles was born. FSC's founding members included people such as the director of the Bank of England; executives from the Smithsonian, Harvard, Yale, Massachusetts Institute of Technology, Carnegie Institute, Princeton University and McGill University; and representatives from the United Nations. Later, a

---

[31] Dr. Charles Nenner, "It's the Cycle, Stupid—Following Market Patterns," *Institutional Investor,* 11/30/11, https://www.institutionalinvestor.com/article/b150zsr0nz9rfq/its-the-cycle-stupid-following-market-patterns

vice president of the United States and billionaire investors would become prominent members.

The research was astonishing. Economic cycles repeat just like months and seasons do. Dewey stumbled on a series of coincidences that were not only financial, but also extended into weather patterns, migration, animal populations, interest rates, business sales, wars and plagues. Cycles not only apply to the economy; they exist throughout nature.

In fact, billionaire and top money manager Paul Tudor Jones was a member of the FSC. I wondered whether this was how he was able to make $100 million in one day by shorting the market on October 19, 1987, when the market dropped 23%. Could cycle knowledge have allowed him to buy massive puts (option contracts) before the biggest one-day decline in our lifetimes? No one predicted it, the computers went haywire that day and program selling kicked in, yet he was prepared and executed a plan that day that made him enormous wealth. He said: *"There are many more deep intellectuals in the business today. That, plus the explosion of information on the Internet, creates an illusion that there is an explanation for everything."*[32] Is he telling us there may be an alternate explanation other than news for why investments move, namely cycles?

The stunning conclusions FSC made are that *energy waves affect business, investments and the financial markets in regularly recurring patterns that make them predictable years in advance.* It seemed too fantastic for me to accept until I began to research quantum physics. As quantum physicist Nikola Tesla explains: *"If you wish to understand the Universe, think in terms of energy, frequency, and vibration."*[33]

I started looking for other people who knew about cycles. In the early 1900s, a cycle researcher named William D. Gann reportedly read cycles and amassed a fortune of $50 million. He

---

[32]Paul Tudor Jones, *Ritholtz.com website,* https://ritholtz.com/2015/05/paul-tudor-jones-13-insights/

[33] Nikola Tesla, "If you want to find the secrets of the universe, think in terms of energy, frequency and vibration," *Goodreads.* https://www.goodreads.com/quotes/361785-if-you-want-to-find-the-secrets-of-the-universe

made 264 profitable trades out of 286 trades in 25 market days. Gann believed in the law of vibration and that stock movements could be determined mathematically using that law:

> *"Through the law of vibration every stock in the market moves in its own distinctive sphere of activities, as to intensity, volume and direction; all the essential qualities of its evolution are characterized in its own rate of vibration. Stocks, like atoms, are centers of energy; therefore, they are controlled mathematically. Stocks create their own field of action and power: power to attract and repel, which principle explains why certain stocks at times lead the market and 'turn dead' at other times. Thus, to speculate scientifically it is absolutely necessary to follow natural law."*[34]

Lest you think this is foolishness, the New York Stock Exchange apparently does not. A painting of Gann hangs there.

Even with Covid-19, we are seeing a 100-year repeating cycle. Did you know there has been a pandemic about every 100 years? In 1720, the Great Plague of Marseille; in 1820, the cholera pandemic in Asia; in 1920, the Spanish flu; and in 2020, the coronavirus. Using that cycle, I was able to tell my VIP Experience members we would be dealing with Covid-19 for three years — the same length of time that past pandemics lasted; a forecast that shocked them at first, but is looking on point.

Probably the most proficient cycle researcher is Martin Armstrong, a self-taught man who stumbled onto cycles by accident when he was a boy. One day, he came across a list of financial panics that occurred between 1683 and 1907. He divided the span of 224 years by the number of panics and found out that, on average, there has been a panic every 8.6 years. He discerned a recurrence of major turning points in the economy and in world affairs that followed a distinct and unwavering 8.6-year rhythm. Six cycles of 8.6 years added up to a long-wave cycle of 51.6 years, which separated such phenomena as Black

[34] "WD Gann Patient Studies Finally Paid Huge Rewards," *Brainyforex*.
http://www.brainyforex.com/gann.html

Friday and the commodity panic of 1920, and the Second and Third Punic Wars.

My jaw dropped when he said 8.6 years is 3,141 days or pi (3.141) times 1,000. Pi is part of the formula to determine the circumference of a circle — the perfect cycle.[35] He developed the Economic Confidence Model, which shows 8.6-year cycles. The 8.6-year wave breaks down into three individual alternating waves with a time duration of 2.15- and 1.075-year periods, making up long and short legs. Six waves of 8.6 years combine into a 51.6-year wave and six waves of the 51.6-year wave combine to form the 309.6-year cycle.

Dr. Nenner said sunspot cycles reminded him of stock market cycles. Perhaps there is a closer relationship than he realizes. According to Dewey and Dakin, authors of *Cycles: The Science of Prediction*:

> *"Now, let us suppose that there are still longer waves in the universe — "Y" waves we may call them. Imagine some of the waves with peaks which come 3½ years apart, others with peaks 9 years apart, 18-1/3 years apart, 54 years apart, and perhaps much farther spaced. It is not inconceivable that these longer waves could directly or indirectly affect the sun, the weather, animals, and human beings, and that just as a red pencil may respond to light waves of only one length, so a particular kind of organism might respond only to Y waves of one particular length."[36]*

This may explain why plants, animals or economic cycles affect one thing and not another.

Armstrong explains that long-term, the pendulum swings between having more government to less government, meaning more private sector, and back from the private sector to having

---

[35] Martin A. Armstrong, "The Business Cycle and the Future," *Armstrong Economics,* 9/26/99, https://www.armstrongeconomics.com/writings/1999-2/the-business-cycle-and-the-future/

[36] Edward R. Dewey & Edwin F. Dakin, *Cycles: The Science of Prediction, 1947.*

more government. He says, *"The flight to quality alternates depending on who is in trouble."*[37] His cycle chart shows a major peak in September of 1929, and we all know that was before a major stock market crash. In 1981, there was a major stock market low before the great bull market began in August 1982. He predicts a final peak is ahead in December of 2032.

Although at times it coincides perfectly with stock market tops and bottoms, this is not meant to be a timing clock. Rather, it is meant to depict international capital flows. *"There is a shift back and forth between PUBLIC and PRIVATE investment trends. For example, the wave that peaked in 1929 was a PRIVATE wave where people had great confidence in the private sector. When the crash came, we turned toward the government creating a more conservative wave of PUBLIC investment where bonds do better than stocks."*[38]

Reportedly, the elite have used knowledge about cycles for generations and kept it among themselves. The Rothschilds, for example, *"had broken up the (stock market) price fluctuations into a series of repeating curves that had been combined and used for forecasting."*[39]

Cycles are Part of Our Daily Lives

Women inherently understand cycles because their bodies demonstrate cycles in a definite way every month. I chuckle when people say they "don't believe in cycles." That is like saying you don't believe in the four seasons. When the new moon is north at 0 degrees, it is the Winter Solstice. In the first quarter, the moon is east at 90 degrees; that is the Spring Equinox. When the moon is full and south at 180 degrees, it is the Summer Solstice. And the last quarter is west at 270 degrees, the Fall Equinox. These are cycles, too.

Cycles exist and are part of our everyday lives. Days of the week are cycles, months are cycles, seasons are cycles. When

---

[37] Martin Armstrong, ArmstrongEconomics.com.
[38] Martin Armstrong, ArmstrongEconomics.com,
https://www.armstrongeconomics.com/models/7219-2/.
[39] Edward R. Dewey & Edwin F. Dakin, *Cycles: The Science of Prediction, 1947.*

someone says they don't believe in cycles, are they saying they don't believe in full moons? Weeks and days? Leap years? Tide schedules? Biorhythms? Heart beats? These are all cycles.

Just as our reference to waves of light is a mathematical reference, not a sensory one, so is our reference to waves in the economy. The waves we talk about are a mathematical record of energies which — so far as people are concerned — appear in their lives as pay cuts or raises, or the courage to buy a new automobile, or the self-denial involved in making the old hat do, or the determination to see that the family moves into another neighborhood before Nellie becomes of school age. Trillions of such daily events, built up from people's decisions and impulses, are the energies that distribute themselves through society.[40]

As Dr. Nenner says, *"In Physics, nothing is random. In Economics, everything is random. They both can't be true."* Laws are universal, so therefore I vote for the physics model — that nothing is random. In fact, nothing in the universe is random; it is all a well-organized, coordinated system that works like a symphony when treated right.

There is also a cycle for every year in a decade. For example, the second year of a decade (a year ending in 2) is often the low. Some interesting cycles are coming up in 2022: It will be 20 years since the 2002 low, 40 years since the 1982 low, 60 years since the 1962 low, 80 years from the 1942 low and 90 years since the 1932 low.

The Cycle of World Reserve Currencies

Earlier I talked about central banks controlling fiat currencies. It has been exactly 50 years since we went off the gold standard and our money became fiat. Fiat means it is not backed by a physical asset. Our dollar bills were once "silver certificates" that represented physical silver, which was the real value, not the paper. Nixon fully disconnected any value from paper currency,

---

[40] Dewey & Dakin, *Cycles: The Science of Prediction*, 1947.

so now our money is reliant on the faith and confidence in the currency and the country that issues it, as well as the strength of the military backing it.

U.S. Secretary of State Henry Kissinger made an agreement with Arab countries that oil would only be purchased in U.S. dollars. That is how it became known as the "petrodollar." Recently, China and Russia have said they will no longer use the U.S. dollar to buy oil. China started an oil exchange that can be traded for gold-backed yuan. If the U.S. dollar loses value by creating too much of it through stimulus programs, it could continue to weaken.

While many other currencies are doing the same thing, it only means the U.S. dollar is like the best house in a bad neighborhood. Fiat currencies don't have a good history and have a fairly regular cycle. Could the US dollar be heading toward the end of a cycle where central bank digital currencies take on a larger role?

According to economist Chris Ferreira, *"The reserve currency transition is a cycle that has typically lasted in history somewhere between 80 to 110 years. Officially, the U.S. dollar has been the reserve currency for 68 years. However, the U.S. dollar was used in trade much before, since the 1920s in fact. That would put the U.S. dollar closer to 90+ years as the reserve currency."* [41] Before the U.S. dollar became the world reserve currency, these countries held that position an average of 95 years, a 95-year cycle: Britain, 105 years; France, 95 years; Netherlands, 80 years; Spain, 110 years; and Portugal, 80 years.

Bubbles and Cycles

I have explained how cycles exist in weather, biology, pandemics, commodities, stocks and money, among other things, and how they are part of nature and repeat at regular intervals. A component of a cycle is the peak, also known as a bubble, in

---

[41] Chris Ferreira, *EconomicReason.com,* World Reserve Currencies: What Happened During Previous Periods of Transition? August 11, 2014.
https://www.economicreason.com/usdollarcollapse/world-reserve-currencies-what-happened-during-previous-periods-of-transition/

which the price has gone through the roof to excessive levels. It seems like everyone who is going to buy has already bought and the bubble is about to pop. Bubbles are part of the cycle and are relatively easy to spot if you know what to look for. However, it is common for people to claim a bubble peak too early, only because the price continues to rise.

Bitcoin's peak in 2017 had all the classic signs of the peak of a bubble. I was able to report about it on a podcast. I remember one person in such desperation to buy into the bitcoin frenzy saying he didn't care if bitcoin was a scam, he couldn't take everyone getting rich but him, and he was going to invest in it, even if he lost all of his money. Talk about crazy. That is the kind of language you hear at bubble peaks.

The emotion behind the fear of missing out (FOMO) is strong. Some people said they were taking out second mortgages to buy bitcoin. A stranger recommended buying bitcoin to my sister at a cocktail party. All classic signs of a top or peak. It reminded me very much of the year 2000 bubble in Internet stocks; the same thing was happening. People were throwing their money into any Internet stock right at the top of the market.

12 Anecdotal Signs of a Bubble

A high price alone is not enough to prove an asset is at a bubble peak; you must have all 12 anecdotal signs of a bubble. Anecdotal just means it is based on personal accounts or observable evidence, rather than calculations or fundamental analysis.

A lot of people are saying that the tech bubble is back and crypto is in a bubble. I don't agree with this because not all of the signs of a bubble are present. A dramatic price increase is not enough to prove a bubble. Many assets have increased in value dramatically and continued to increase for years. Crypto is too despised by the media and too unknown by the public to be in a bubble. At the peak of a bubble everyone, even the media, will be singing its praises.

The 12 anecdotal signs of a bubble are:

1. Everyone owns the asset.

2. The price rises above what it is worth to a level that is so extreme, it is indefensible.

3. So many people have done well investing in it that they recommend it to everyone.

4. Everyone favors the asset. Even financial magazine covers are touting it.

5. No "bears" (believers that it will decline in value) are left.

6. There is a belief it will only go up and will never go down, for any number of reasons.

7. People quit their jobs to invest and make money at it full-time.

8. TV shows are created about it.

9. It is a common subject to talk about at cocktail parties.

10. If you aren't an investor in it, you finally do invest, even though you think you shouldn't.

11. The FOMO emotion is so strong, people will buy at any price.

12. Wall Street has made a fortune selling it to everyday investors.

We are not even close to this level of acceptance in cryptocurrencies. Quite the opposite. Financial news channels are saying the bull market in crypto is "near the end." Haters are still hating it. Every day on Twitter, some stock analyst calls crypto a bubble. Wall Street has not even begun selling it to everyday investors.

Nope.

Not even close. It is too hated, too early and too misunderstood. What is going on is an adoption of a new currency — the ability to invest in early-stage technology companies undergoing a revolution — and it is global.

The Bottom Line

Understanding cycles is a remarkable way to look at the past and the future in terms of investing. Few people realize how important cycles are. Now, this way of looking at the world has been opened up to you.

Leap into the Quantum Age

Make a list of all the cryptocurrencies you currently have. Create a strategy for how long you want to hold onto them. Write down why you bought them and how long you plan to hold onto them. Put it away and anytime you have an urge to sell, bring it out and reread it.

Chapter 15
Why People Lose Their Wealth

"To keep the wealth you create, follow the Six Steps to Maintaining Wealth."

We all dream of being lottery winners. The thought of having millions suddenly at your disposal to buy whatever you want is a common, seductive fantasy. If only you could have enough money to buy your heart's desire. If only you had enough money to buy your dream home. If only you had enough money to help others. The idea of no lack of money is a heady one. Imagine having the money to buy anything you can think of. No limits, no shortage, no end to what you could have, do or be. It is intoxicating to think about.

However, the reality is much different from our money fantasies. The reality is that most people who have sudden wealth will have spent all of their money within five years. "Instead of finding themselves in the lap of luxury, 70% of people who come into sudden money are broke within a few years," according to the National Endowment for Financial Education. The Certified Financial Planner Board of Standards says nearly a third of lottery winners

declare bankruptcy.[42]

It is called Sudden Wealth Syndrome (SWS). It happens to lottery winners, sellers of businesses, wealthy divorcées, professional athletes, successful actors and actresses, inheritors of millions, etc. Anytime you have a big increase in money, you are susceptible to becoming a victim of SWS. That is why it is

---

[42] National Endowment for Financial Education, 6/17/21, https://www.nefe.org/news/2018/01/research-statistic-on-financial-windfalls-and-bankruptcy.aspx

also estimated that 78% of professional athletes, 60% of NBA players and 99% of gamblers have no money left in a few years.[43]

Is it the money's fault? No. It is human behavior, lack of financial education and human psychology that are behind the problems with money. If you take an addict and give them more drugs, are they going to change their behavior? No; it is just going to make their situation worse.

It is no different with money. Take a person who is not good at managing $20,000 a year, $50,000 a year, $100,000 a year or $500,000 a year and give them more money. Is it going to solve their problems? If they don't handle less money well, how are they going to handle more money well? But it goes beyond that, because even responsible people with money have a problem when getting more. Let's look at what I believe are some of the causes.

Habits and Beliefs

We know that saving can be hard for some people. In general, it has become a habit for people to spend all of their income every month. The more money you make, theoretically, the easier it is to save, but not if you are a consumer who is trying to appear successful by having an expensive home, cars and vacations. Trying to "look" successful is called "keeping up with the Joneses" and is a never-ending treadmill. Some people are notoriously guilty of spending all of their income and presumably this is because they need to "look successful."

When you make a lot of money, it is easy to spend a lot of money because it is there in your account. You work hard and want to reward yourself, so you buy a new car. The car depreciates by 50% in the first three years, so from an investment or net-worth perspective, it was a bad investment. Eating out in expensive restaurants, going on expensive vacations, living in a big house — it all costs money. Add to that the expense of children and paying for their education and, well, there is not

---

[43] Marilyn Smith, SportsDevotee.com website, https://www.sportsdevotee.com/being-broke-after-playing-sports/

much money left over to invest and create real wealth ... unless you consciously follow the *Wealth Building Formula (McT)™*.

When some people come into a lot of money without much effort, they are inclined to see it as something to use for a spending spree. Their first thoughts are what they can buy with it, not how to invest it. Friends and family may be aware of their good fortune and money may be asked for or demanded. Already they are on the path to losing it all and having nothing left in five years. That is how it happens and why it is so common.

They also might want to see what it feels like to spend and live like a millionaire. I have seen people take an inheritance and say they want to blow it, because they want to see what it feels like to do that. Afterward, of course, they regret it. Blowing through money irresponsibly wasn't such a great feeling after all.

But what if you are a financially responsible person? Will you still lose the money? Sometimes, yes. You have other issues to deal with, like fear, lack of knowledge and lack of a team of financial advisors.

Subconsciously, we all have money beliefs. Some people have a fear of money, so they get rid of it. It is not conscious, but they can't seem to keep money in their checking account. As soon as it comes in, it goes out, even if they are typically "responsible" with money.

You can also have a lack of knowledge about finances and how to invest, so you might make some poor decisions, like in our chapter about what to do with $25,000. Those people aren't bad people, but they are thinking that putting money in a bank account is a smart decision or buying a brand-new car or giving it to your kids is a good decision. They have a lot to learn about money. *The right way to think about money is to get it working harder for you.*

There may also be a lack of team of advisors and oversight. When you come into a lot of money, you need advice — a lot of it. You need tax advice and to prepare for paying any taxes due or filing estate paperwork if you inherited it due to a death. You need investment advice to know how to preserve it and grow it; legal advice to create a will to pass it on. You might need other consultants as well, such as banking, lending, insurance, etc. You might need a personal assistant to help you manage multiple properties, cars, jet charter memberships, etc. With money comes responsibility and sometimes complexity. Having a team of knowledgeable advisors really helps.

Of course, you might not have these issues to deal with, but just in case some mindset blocks are lurking in your subconscious that you are not aware of, I recommend you use my affirmations to change any limiting beliefs or bad habits that might keep you from staying wealthy. After all, you have just come into money, which conflicts with your self-image and may be outside your comfort zone, so you need to start seeing yourself as a wealthy person. Create a new self-image that coincides with your new wealth and remove any mindset blocks that keep you from seeing yourself in your new reality. Otherwise, your subconscious will lead you to reverberate back to your old image of having money struggles and limitations, and you will subconsciously recreate that reality. Consider implementing these five steps to make sure you maintain your newfound wealth.

Next Steps to Maintaining New Wealth

1. ***Work on Creating a New Wealthy Mindset.*** Mindset always comes first, because it is the most important and affects us the most, but it is also the step that people ignore the most. Why? Because your beliefs are subconscious — you aren't aware you have them. You are thinking logically, but emotions are driving your car. Creating a new self-image, of course, requires affirmations to change subconscious beliefs. What is an affirmation you might try? How about: *I am a multi-millionaire and I always will be. My name is _____.*

     Another version of this step is to say it three times, putting emphasis on a different word each time. The first time, put emphasis on the "I," as in "*I* am a multi-millionaire." Next time, emphasize "am" and the third time, emphasize "multi-millionaire." Pay attention and see if one version makes you feel a tug from your subconscious. That may be the area where you need to increase your belief, so you don't self-sabotage.)

Here are some affirmations, sandwiched with already-true statements such as your name, to repeat daily and change money blocks you may have:

I am wealthy inside and out.
My name is _____.

I am comfortable with having money and making financial decisions.
My name is _____.

Being wealthy and staying wealthy is my new reality.
My name is _____.

I am smart and responsible with money, and I make good decisions that keep me wealthy.
My name is _____.

My wealth keeps growing and multiplying.
My name is _____.

My wealth is a good thing that benefits me and others.
My name is _____.

2. *Don't Measure Yourself by Money.* People can easily get caught up in comparing themselves against other people with money. One couple has multiple homes and are worth millions of dollars, yet they always feel broke. They compare themselves to billionaires and never measure up. Do you see how comparing yourself makes you feel less than? It sounds foolish, but these are the "head trips" that people with new money have. Unrealistic comparisons happen when they become wealthy and compare their wealth to others, especially to the richest people in the world. Stop comparing!

3. *Assemble a Team.* Hiring a tax advisor is something you want to do immediately. Before spending or investing, you need to find out how much tax you will owe. Many newly rich people have not considered the taxes due and have gotten into trouble with the IRS by not getting this taken care of in the beginning.

Next, hire an investment advisor. An investment advisor is best when recommended by someone with money. Don't call an investment firm and don't accept an advisor who is pursuing you. Go with someone who is recommended by a happy customer. When you are talking with the advisor, make sure you talk about money moving in cycles and peaking in bubbles, so you are considering all economic cycles and preparing for rising inflation, stock market peaks and troughs, interest rate changes, etc.

Don't just invest for today. You need to think about how cycles can change so you can invest in any climate. For example, interest rates peaked at around 18% in 1982 and declined from there to near-zero interest rates today. The pendulum is likely to swing back, and interest rates will increase for the next 40 years. You need to take this into account in your investing plans. Inflation will also reappear even though inflation has been supposedly less than 2% per year (if measured properly, it would show it has been much higher, but that is another story). Plan for higher inflation and make investment choices that are looking forward to the future cycles, not backward to past cycles.

After your investments are in motion, hire an attorney to create a will and, if necessary, trusts to avoid estate taxes and leave your assets in proper vehicles to protect them for future generations.

Find a good insurance professional who can provide life insurance to pay any estate taxes in the cheapest way possible. My preferred versions of insurance are Universal Life, a combination of term insurance and a money market account, or just plain term insurance. I am not a fan of whole life insurance.

4. **Create a List of Wants.** Since spending is a problem when you have sudden wealth, I recommend you write a list of purchases you plan to make before you buy. The key word is "plan." Planning will keep you from impulse spending. It is easy to get caught up in the moment and want to buy something, and later you wonder what you were thinking. By writing it down, you are spending time thinking about what you truly desire, and it can help you avoid impulse buys.

Make a list and stick to it. If you want to only allow yourself to spend "x" amount of dollars, that is fine; everyone has pent-up demand and a list of things they want to buy right away. Give yourself leeway of 5% to "blow" on what you want, whether it is a new car, vacation or house; whatever. Stop spending after you have what is on your list. Now it is time to replenish the funds you spent.

5. **Have a Plan to Invest and Replenish Funds.** Since you are spending some of your new wealth, what is your plan to generate money and replace the money you spend? This is one of the most-overlooked steps with sudden millionaires. They have a plan to spend, but they don't have a plan to replenish the money spent. That is why the money disappears. They are spending principal with no plan to generate more. It is not wise to spend principal. It is wise to spend only the interest generated by the principal invested, but again, sudden millionaires are eager to spend the entire inheritance, new wealth or lottery win. They view the money as a "spending account" that they can spend until it is gone. Please understand: If you spend your principal, it will all be gone!

Work with your financial advisor to diversify and invest 95% of the money. Think about creating a well-diversified portfolio with a wide range of investments. What investments are high-priced right now and have less potential to appreciate? Which investments are low right now and have a lot of potential to appreciate? What is the right mix or allocation of assets, so you are not overly invested in one asset class? You don't want to have everything in stock, bonds or real estate. Of course, you want to pay off debt and not take on new debt, but you already knew that.

Think about how you are going to replenish the money you spent — through income streams like rental income, dividend income, royalties, capital gains, etc. When you are meeting with your financial advisor, ask what investments are income generators and what investments provide capital growth. Since you already have wealth, you don't need to be taking a lot of risk. You can allow yourself a lower rate of return as long as you are outpacing the annual rate of inflation. Treasury bonds that keep pace with inflation, or Treasury Inflation-Protected Securities (TIPS), may work for part of your portfolio.

You might think that a billion dollars is so much money it could never be whittled away and lost. Think again. Patricia Kluge received a billion-dollar settlement when she divorced her husband. She considered herself a wine connoisseur and decided to buy a vineyard and start a winery. She didn't have any business experience and made some decisions that cost her a lot of money. Long story short, she ended up losing the vineyard, her mansion, jewelry and all of her possessions, and went bankrupt.

Yes, it is possible to obtain a billion dollars and go broke. That is why I'm urging you to have reliable sources of multiple income streams or growth investments to replace the money you spend.

Calculate Your Net Worth Annually

You should know your net worth and keep track of the direction it is moving in.

What is your net worth, and how do you calculate it? Your net worth is the sum of your assets minus your liabilities. An asset is everything you own: your house, car, boat, furniture, clothes, investment account, 401(k), IRA, pension, rental properties, stocks, bonds, art, Certificates of Deposit, and checking/savings accounts. It is everything that has a positive value or that you could get money for. Liabilities are debt: credit cards, student loans, car loans, boat loans, business loans, home mortgage and so on — everything that you owe.

Add up all your assets. Now add up all your liabilities. Next, subtract your liabilities from your assets; that equals your net worth. It looks like this: Assets – Liabilities = Net Worth. You can increase your net worth by adding assets that can substantially increase in value over the long term, such as real estate, stocks, crypto or a business. The other way to increase your net worth is to pay off any debt.

What will decrease your net worth? Buying assets that depreciate, such as cars, motorcycles, motorhomes, three-wheeler ATVs, jet skis, boats, clothing and furniture. While these are assets, they will be worth less every year, so they are actually decreasing your net worth. Your best financial decisions will be those that will increase your net worth long-term as opposed to a new car that will depreciate in value each year.

The Bottom Line

The right mindset does not stop with obtaining wealth. It is also critical in *keeping* your wealth. Having the right mindset and a smart plan can protect you from losing what you have worked so hard to build as well as what drops in your lap serendipitously.

Leap into the Quantum Age

1. Are you already thinking of ways to spend your cryptocurrency growth? Are those things going to make you happy? Are they worth killing your golden goose? Do you have a plan to replenish what you spend?

2. Make a list of everything you want to buy, but don't act on it. In 30 days, look at what you wrote and see what you don't want anymore. Has your opinion changed?

Chapter 16
Where Would You Invest $25k?

"If you don't know how to invest $25,000 well, will you do better with $2.5 million?"

Since you may find yourself with a lot more money, and I believe you will hold your cryptos and have avalanches of abundance, how good are you at handling it? Recently, I read a post on Facebook that asked, "What would you do with an extra $25,000?" The answers astounded me because they reflected a fundamental lack of understanding about money. While I'm sure you are good with money, in this chapter, we will review choices you have and explain the pros and cons of each choice.

Opportunity Cost

You have choices to make with money. There is an Opportunity Cost (OC) to every decision you make about money. If you decide to invest in the stock market or pay down debt, there is an opportunity cost to each decision. If you decide to spend money instead of saving it, there is an opportunity cost. OC itself isn't good or bad, but the choices you make while considering the OC make them a good decision or not.

While many people have the impression there is only one way to look at finances, there are actually many differing opinions about how to handle money that often conflict with each other. The financial expert who has filed bankruptcy in the past is going to advocate for having zero debt. The expert who built wealth using real estate is going to promote the benefits of using debt to buy real estate and build wealth. Others think being smart with money involves budgeting.

My perspective is that you move your finances and net worth closer to financial freedom by investing your money. Investing is growing your money and getting your money to compound and multiply. Many wealthy people didn't get that way by earning high wages; in fact, fewer than 33% of millionaires have ever earned more than $100,000 annually. And it is common for some of the highest-wage earners, to have a lot of debt and not much net worth. Why? It could be because they aren't focused on investing.

As we have been seeing throughout this book, investing is what will increase your net worth, grow your wealth, and allow you to retire and have financial freedom. Yet, investing is not taught in school or by financial advisors. They do it for you, not teach you how to do it for yourself. If your parents didn't know or show you how to do it, it can be a bit of a steep learning curve.

One reason is that the stock market has its own language and if you don't learn it, you may as well be listening to Greek. CAGRs, alpha, beta, gamma, options, p/e ratios, Sharpe ratios, margin, ETFs, mutual funds, technical analysis, fundamental analysis, etc. — the list of financial terminology goes on and on. If you don't know what the words mean, it can be nearly impossible to navigate the field. That is why I am here to speak plain English, remove the jargon and show you what to pay attention to so you can grow your money.

You have choices for what to do with your money. You can choose to spend, save or invest it. How do you know which is best? What if we just look at the building blocks of wealth-building that work for all wealth-building, and then I show you a simple and efficient way to multiply your money?

In my opinion, the right OC when investing is usually the one that will compound your money the best. Some people will disagree with that statement because they believe it should be related to the level of risk you want to take. It is not a 100% win-or-lose situation. It is a question of whether you want your money to grow at 6% or 10% annually. If it grew at 10%, would you be able to handle a greater fluctuation in value? Is it worth it?

Yes, because if your money grows at 4% annually, it will take 18 years to double your money. If you want your money to compound at 10% annually, it will double in 7.2 years. If you are investing for financial freedom, you want your money to double in fewer years, obviously.

Why would you invest money so it intentionally compounds more slowly? Because you answered a question on an advisor's risk questionnaire by saying you didn't like risk, which is essentially the fluctuation of your money. If you answered the questionnaire with "I don't like risk," you will cause your asset allocation to be slanted toward investments that grow slower — at 6% instead of 10%. If you say you can't handle as much risk (fluctuation), then you will be invested in more conservative portfolios, which means you will probably have slower growth, and it will take longer to attain financial freedom. You are ensuring that over the long term, you will have less money!

Rather than set up your portfolio to compound at 6%, when a 10% average is possible in stocks (not guaranteed, but the long-run track record), perhaps you need additional education about how to handle the increased risk. In my opinion, women in particular need to understand the repercussions of their answers on risk questionnaires. By understanding the ramifications of your answers about risk, now you know you are saying you want a slower path to financial freedom.

Making Good Choices

How did people answer the question on Facebook about where they would invest a $25,000 windfall? Here were the responses, with my comments in parentheses:

- Buy a car (a depreciating asset guaranteed to be worth less in three years).

- Pay off high-interest debt (a definite possibility to consider, but how did the debt get there in the first place and has the overspending stopped?).

- Put it in a savings account (likely the worst answer. There is virtually no interest earned in a savings account, and it is losing purchasing power each year because it is earning less than the inflation rate).

- Fund an IRA or Roth IRA (a good choice because at least you can invest it and get it growing for you).

- Make a down payment on a house and get a 15-year mortgage (that means they are buying a very expensive asset and committing more of their cash flow than they would pay on a 30-year mortgage, which will result in them not being able to save as much for retirement).

Not one person said they would invest in cryptocurrency or digital assets. That means we are early, and most people don't even have it on their radar as an option. Meanwhile, institutions and hedge funds that manage money for the wealthy, private wealth and family offices are all rushing to add at least a 3% to 5% allocation to cryptocurrency, blockchain and Internet of value investments. I will talk about that in a moment, but first let's look at each choice from the Facebook responses.

Buying a car with $25k. In three years, your $25,000 would be worth about half, or $12,500. That's not good.

Savings account. You are losing purchasing power of at least 2% per year, so in five years, your money can only buy $22,500 of goods and services. That's not good either.

Invested in an IRA and bought an index fund. You would have an opportunity to grow your money at 10% long-term rates of return. In the last five years, the S & P 500 has averaged 15% per year. If it did that for the next five years, your money will have doubled to $50,283. Well done!

But what if you had invested 95% of your $25,000 windfall in the S & P 500 and just 5% of it in cryptocurrency? The 95% is $23,750 and invested in stocks; it would have grown to $47,769. The 5% invested in the Bitwise 100 largest cryptocurrencies for the last five years would have grown 6,000% — to $75,000! Added together, $23,750 and $75,000 is a total of $122,769. *Very* well done!

Do you see how someone with an understanding of compounding and investing is going to make better decisions that will advance them the most toward financial freedom? One person has a depreciated car; the other has multiplied their windfall almost five times.

In 20 years, the new car is worth next to nothing, the cash $25,251.19 (less purchasing power lost due to inflation), you could have saved interest on debt, the stocks would be worth $409,163, and stocks/5% cryptos would be worth who knows how much? We used real numbers for 5-year compounding, but we don't have returns for an index of cryptos with 20-year returns. Clearly on a 5-year basis using real returns, the stocks plus 5% in cryptos was the clear winner. I suspect it would be for the 20-year period as well. We shall see.

Financial literacy is the most important issue causing the wealth gap. The answer is knowing what to do with your money and how to invest it well. Fortunately, cryptocurrencies are providing a solution.

The Bottom Line

The "Where Would You Invest 25K?" exercise is very powerful because it is so concrete. It helps you solidify your decisions and understand opportunity cost is very real.

Leap into the Quantum Age

Take a close look at the chart in this chapter. Where would you invest $25k? Based on this chart, what does your $25k investment look like? Be as specific as you can.

Chapter 17
The New Reality for Millennials, GenX and Boomers

"All generations are experiencing a wealth gap. Cryptocurrencies will help close it."

When students go to journalism school, they are trained to write articles or press releases that answer the questions of who, what, when, where and why. So far in this book, I have spent my time talking about what, when, where and why. I have also made the statement that anyone can create wealth with digital assets and find financial freedom if they follow specific steps and incorporate the wealth-building formula based on money, time and — most importantly — compounding.

Now I want to share some perspectives on who.

The truth is that individuals are different, and they have been shaped by their generations; what they have experienced in their personal lives; and the political, economic and social events of their times. Our shorthand for categorizing these differences is millennials, GenX and baby boomers.

What is the new reality for these generations? What specific challenges do they have with their mindset that can affect tapping into the explosion of opportunity for wealth-building? How do they perceive risk? What do they care about, and how does that affect their financial decision-making?

As you read this, I would like you to think about your own generation, as well as others. We all live in multi-generational families. Our financial decisions may be linked to guiding our children or protecting our parents. We need to understand our own reality, and also how other generations are affected. As more serious investors are involved in cryptocurrencies and more millionaires are being created, people

— no matter what age — are getting in the game. The trick is to not let your gender or age stop you from acting now.

Before we talk about generations, let's take a short detour and look at women and wealth. Women have long been excluded from the investment world, but that began changing in the last decades of the 20th century as they became more involved. Still, the advice they were given financially was generally about reducing spending rather than smart investing. Today, all of that is changing, and cryptocurrency is one major reason.

While women still make up a small percentage of cryptocurrency investors, that has increased dramatically in the last few years. A 2020 Greyscale Investor study found that only 15 percent of bitcoin investors are women, but 47 percent surveyed said they would consider investing in bitcoin.[44] According to research by CoinMarketCap, Q1 2020 saw a 43.24% growth in women investing in cryptocurrency compared to the same time the previous year.[45] Interestingly, the study also showed that a surge in women investors was happening in Latin America, with an 80 percent quarter-on-quarter growth.

In a survey by BDC Consulting on women in crypto, a third of those involved said the main event pushing them to consider cryptocurrencies was conversations with partners, friends and colleagues.[46] The survey also discovered 44% of respondents invested in cryptocurrencies to gain financial independence. BDC speculated that the reason that women are drawn to cryptocurrency investing to obtain financial freedom is that it removes barriers experienced by women and provides simpler ways to access money.

Unfortunately, women are still being excluded (which is one of the reasons I have written this book). Those surveyed by BDC felt that crypto

[44] Grayscale Investor Study, https://grayscale.com/wp-content/uploads/2021/01/1020-2020-bitcoin-investor-study.pdf
[45] CoinMarketCap website, https://files.coinmarketcap.com/static/marketing/according-to-coinmarketcap-2020-q1.pdf
[46] BDC Consulting, https://bdc.consulting/insights/cryptocurrency/bitcoin-under-female-thumb-global-study-women-cryptosphere

Information and spaces are made by men for men. But women are changing this dynamic, particularly Millennial women. One in four customers who traded crypto so far in 2021 on the Robinhood Markets platform is a woman, according to Christine Brown, chief operating officer. Over the past two years, digital trading platform, Toro Group Ltd. said the number of female crypto traders in the U.S. on its platform jumped by half, to about 20% of all users in the U.S.

Women are catching up. But what does investing look like to people in different generations? What is their new reality? Let's start with a really interesting question: What amount of money makes you feel financially comfortable?

Money Comfort Among Generations

Each generation says there is a different amount you need to be considered financially comfortable in 2021. For millennials, it is $618,000. For GenX, it is $717,000. For baby boomers, it is $609,000. To put that in context, U.S. households had an average net worth of $748,800 before the pandemic. In terms of what it takes to feel wealthy, around $1.9 million is what most Americans thought they needed. Not coincidentally, the estimated amount to "feel wealthy" was also the target amount for retirement.

According to the Federal Reserve 2019 Survey of Consumer Finances, the median or midpoint net worth of all families was much lower: just $121,700 in 2019. The median means half are above and half are below compared to the average, which is all net worths added together and divided by the number you are averaging. The median is very telling: Half the people have a net worth below $121,700 and half the people have a net worth above $121,700. That tells us a lot more about the reality of people's net worth rather than averaging it, because people who are very wealthy are going to bring the average up. When you use the median and you know half of net worths are below $121,700, that tells you we need to do a much better job in financial literacy, education and investing.

Every Generation is Worried about Retirement

While retirement worries start getting much stronger when people approach their 40th birthday, every generation expresses concerns about retirement — and for good reason. Social Security alone will not cover the average American's monthly expenses. Social Security on average provides $1,430 per month, while the average monthly expenditure in retirement is approximately $5,000 a month.

To have $60,000 of income for 30 years at current interest rates of around 3% (that is being generous), you will need $2 million. In the past, we had bonds that helped provide predictable streams of income. Now, we have crypto and the ability to be our own bank. Cryptocurrencies can provide the 6% to 8% income that used to be provided by bonds when we had normal interest rates. All you need to do is deposit or "stake" crypto to activate it. We are fortunate to be living in a time when we can generate these low-risk income streams by alternate methods.

If you have $1.5 million invested at 6%, it could generate $90,000 of annual income and that is enough to cover average costs in retirement. The nice thing is that in this example, we are not spending principal, so as long as you can earn 6% and live on $90,000 a year, you won't be invading principal. In the case of inflation rising, that might mean that interest rates on crypto rise above 6% and/or you could dip into principal a little to make up the difference. At least you have options for how to handle it.

Both millennials and GenXers need to start a Roth IRA; this allows you to put $6,000 annually (since you are under age 50) into the account and not have to pay tax on any gains during accumulation while it is invested. When you reach age 59-½, you can withdraw the funds tax-free.

Millennials and Wealth-building

Gen Y, or millennials, were born between 1981 and 1994-96. They are currently between 25 and 40 years old and number 72.1 million in the U.S. Gen Y.1 is a subgroup of millennials who are 25-29 years old. Currently, 88% of millennials invest their money, citing their motivation as to plan for their futures. Despite this, only 55% of them feel confident about their money management skills, according to Clutch, the leading B2Bratings and reviews platform.[47] Only 45% are investing to build a retirement fund. While some millennials invest in traditional or Roth individual retirement accounts (IRAs) (29%), stocks (25%) and mutual funds (14%), the majority chose 401(k) plans (53%).

Millennials make up the largest adopters of digital assets as an investment strategy. Researchers believe one reason is because millennials grew natively with mobile and crypto. They understand digital wallets and treasure chests which are part of games like Fortnite and Minecraft.

Affluent millennials are ahead of their time and already smartly invested in cryptocurrencies: 47% of young investors who own at least $1 million in their crypto portfolios responded that they had invested at least one-quarter of their wealth, according to a survey conducted by the Spectrem Group.[48]

Additionally, younger Millennials may not have credit cards or bank accounts, so they leverage crypto wallets to conduct trades and transactions. Younger millennials also are not as concerned about saving for retirement at this point in their lives as older generations. Remember when I said the need starts kicking in the most around age 40? They are willing to take more risks with the hopes of winning big.

For older millennials, their generation has lived through their adult lives bookended by financial disasters, first the 2008 financial crisis, then the pandemic. They have had to contend with spiraling costs for college and burgeoning student debt. Millennials are the best-educated so far and value flexible schedules, free time and meaningful work. They tend to spend more versus save, but still have the goal to retire early. I recommend that they start investing early to maximize the time

[47] Anna Peck, *Clutch.co website,* 2/1/21, https://clutch.co/accounting/resources/smart-money-tips-investment-beginners
[48] Robert Frank, *CNBC website,* 6/10/21, https://www.cnbc.com/2021/06/10/millennial-millionaires-have-large-share-of-wealth-in-crypto-cnbc-survey-.html

to compound. Remember my examples of how easy it was to accumulate a fortune the more years you have to compound? If you are a millennial, put that into practice *now*: Start saving and investing *now*. Even if you can only invest $25 a month, it will pay off dramatically over your lifetime and make a huge difference. Do the same as soon as your children are born: Start saving from day one.

Savings has never been easier due to the apps that are available. I am sure more will be developed, and everything eventually will be automated. Online services like mint.com can help you with automatic investing, paying bills and keeping track of all your accounts in one place. Since ETFs became popular during your lifetime, passive investing trends are likely to continue. It is important to watch the expenses connected with investments and use index ETFs to minimize them.

When it comes to buying a home, millennials are at a disadvantage because home prices have escalated so much. Millennials have much lower home ownership rates than GenXers and baby boomers at the same age. That could be from putting off major life events like getting married and having a family.

Millennials are keener to rent than buy or live a more nomadic lifestyle when single by serial housesitting or staying in an Airbnb. While I cannot predict what a home will cost in 10 years, I can tell you that it is a good forced-savings plan no matter what home prices do. If you borrow $300,000 to buy a home, that will no longer be debt once you have paid off the mortgage but instead will be equity and real wealth in your net-worth asset column. Think of any mortgage as a future asset because as you pay off the debt, it becomes equity. If you have decided not to buy a home and just rent, remember it may save you money in the short term, but you will not get the advantage of forced savings and creating an asset.

Beyond home-sharing, millennials may want to share cars, too. This means you will be able to save significant money since you do not have to pay thousands to buy a car, insure it or pay for repairs.

One of the smartest investments you can make is to spend a few hundred dollars a year on term life insurance that can be used by your heirs to pay off credit-card debt, college debt or mortgage debt, or set up a college fund for your kids in the event of your untimely death.

Millennials care about changing the world. A special account can help you with making charitable contributions: a Donor Advised Fund (DAF). It has a terrible name, but it is a wonderful account. When you donate money to your DAF, you get an immediate tax deduction. Then you can donate the money to your favorite IRS-approved charities over time. This allows you to "front-load" your charitable deductions in a high-income year to reduce your taxable income.

For example, if you donate $5,000 (the minimum to open a DAF account) to it, you have made a charitable donation for tax purposes. You can then choose to donate a portion or all of it to as many charities as you like, while your assets in the fund grow tax-free. It is like having your own mini-charitable foundation. You choose the charities from your account's website, select a dollar amount to donate and the administrators will send the check to the charity.

It is true that 33% of millennials over age 30 are still living at home. That is astounding. I believe it shows that the cost of living is beyond their means to live on their own. Wages available to earn are too low, and rents are too high. They also have record-breaking levels of student debt. Therefore, it is less expensive to live with Mom and Dad, and ideally save money for a down payment on a house or at least a damage deposit on an apartment. It is a travesty that college-educated young people cannot afford to live on their own.

Saving more money in a bank savings account earning .05% annual interest isn't the answer. Investing and compounding is. Wealth is only created when it is invested in an appreciating asset. That is why 401(k)s have been such a success, and there are 365,000 401(k) millionaires. They are taking money from their paychecks and investing in a money engine: the stock market. Since the stock market averages about a 10% return over the long term, it is possible for a person to enter the workforce, contribute $3,100 per year for 35 years, and accumulate $1 million in their lifetime at a 10% return. Of course, with cryptocurrency investments in your portfolio, you could also do a lot better than that.

That seems very doable to me, but you have to know to do it and start early. Again, we don't teach people that. You have to have someone tell you or figure it out on your own. With 401(k)s making it so easy to deduct money from your paycheck, you probably won't even miss the money that doesn't make it into your bank account.

The irony is that many millennials hope to inherit money from their GenX or baby boomer parents, who have had the benefit of 401(k)s compounding for years, record high home prices and high wages. But not so fast. End-of-life expenses are so high that they can eat through a seven- or eight-figure potential inheritance very easily. Nursing home care or round-the-clock home health care is very expensive — upward of $100,000 annually or more.

Depending on how the parents die and the cause of death, even a family's substantial estate can dwindle to a much smaller amount by the time it is passed on. The parents of younger millennials also may be struggling saving for their own retirement or even paying off their children's student loans.

GenX and Wealth-building

GenX was born between 1965 and 1979/80 and is currently between 41–56 years old. They make up 65.2 million of the U.S. population. GenXers have the highest after-tax income and spend the most. However, they save the most (16%), more than GenYers (10%) and baby boomers (10%). Surprisingly, GenXers are spending more on personal insurance and pensions, even more than boomers.

GenXers are in a similar position to baby boomers, although most are still working and bringing in an income. GenX is resource-strapped while trying to raise a family, pay off student debt and take care of aging parents. Their children, GenZ (ages

6–24), are watching the struggles of all the other generations and trying to figure out what to do to avoid debt.

GenXers tend to be more conservative with money and are excellent savers. They are more into work/life balance, value experiences over having more things, and may even want to retire early and/or take a sabbatical to experience new places.

For GenXers, this is a great time to move forward with developing ideas for their own businesses. They also need to focus on staying healthy since they could live a very long time. In a world of potentially combining humans and robots, regeneration of limbs, super healing chambers, free energy for homes and cars, colonies on Mars, flying cars, teleporting, and a host of new technologies, staying healthy means experiencing one or more things that right now seem like a pipe dream, but will be reality and commonplace.

Social media has been a boon to both millennials and GenXers because you can become an influencer online. If you can build a large-enough following, brands will pay you to market their products, or you can become an affiliate and earn a commission on each sale. Instagram and YouTube have created income for GenXers with a voice and audience.

In addition, for both groups, whole industries that have not even been created yet that will need talented workers. Even if robots and artificial intelligence mean fewer low-paying jobs, I think overall they will create more jobs. New uses, transition teams and thought leaders will be needed.

GenXers are in line for some of the largest wealth transfers in history as baby boomers die out and leave them money. This means they need to be very savvy about investing. It also means they have to step up their game on cryptocurrency investing. A study from Piplsay found that 49% of millennials polled own cryptocurrency compared to 38% of GenXers and 13% of GenZ. Millennials are also more likely to adopt the investment as a form of payment, with 53% saying they are "very likely" to purchase products or services with crypto, vs. 40% of GenX polled and just 7% of GenZ.[49]

Baby Boomers and Wealth-building

Baby boomers were born between 1946 and 1964. They're currently between 57–75 years old and number 71.6 million in the U.S. Not surprisingly since they are the oldest, they are spending 9.5% of their total spending on healthcare.

Not surprisingly, tech-resistant older investors who are millionaires are not fond of digital assets — 83% of them do not believe in the crypto market and have none of their wealth in it. The real data among older rich people show that only one in every 10 keeps more than 10% of their funds in cryptocurrencies.

While baby boomers are managing retirement, life expectancies are on the rise, so some are outliving their retirement funds, experiencing declining pensions and worried about the dwindling Social Security system. Many boomers believe you should take care of children by helping them while you are alive rather than plan to leave an inheritance. There is no right answer; it is up to each individual how to spend their estate.

Boomers have the challenge of running out of time because they have not been able to save enough, and they are living so much longer. The concern of outliving their money is real. Before the pandemic, the fastest-growing demographic was people living longer than age 100. If you are going to retire at age 65 and live another 40 years, are you prepared for that? I do not think most boomers are. That is a long time to have to provide income, especially with the low interest rates we have currently.

Like GenXers, younger boomers are also members of the "sandwich generation," which means they have to deal with college funding and taking care of their aging parents at the same time — plus save for retirement. All three take a large amount of money out of your savings. If your parents have not saved or

---

[49] *Piplsay website,* 5/19/21, https://piplsay.com/the-great-crypto-rush-how-are-americans-investing-in-it/

insured themselves, it can be expensive to care for them and the responsibility may fall on your shoulders.

You are going to have to get creative to find additional sources of income. Even Social Security has raised the retirement age for full benefits from age 65 to age 67, and they will continue to raise it. That is why it is important to spend time thinking about creating multiple streams of income that can last your entire lifetime. As I discussed earlier, my mom owned a 10-unit apartment building that provided her with a handsome income after age 65. She managed it herself until well into her 90s. I think it helped keep her young because it was like a part-time job. It kept her mind active and gave her something to do.

Creating an online business is a great way for Boomers to continue to generate income into their retirement years. Start working on that now and reap the benefits for the rest of your life. If you can have both investing and owning a business working for you, you are maximizing your wealth-building potential.

I also think retiring to a less-expensive city is a trend that will continue. Many boomers have a lot of equity locked up in their homes. Moving to a smaller home or condo is a good decision, and the extra money you do not spend on your new, smaller home can go toward your retirement savings.

I sold my large home after my husband died and moved to our smaller second home. It was a huge relief not to have to deal with the high maintenance of taking care of a large house and yard. Managing roofers, gardeners, tree trimmers, painters, pest exterminators, pond cleaners and window washers just got exhausting. Life is much simpler in a gated community where the care of the common grounds is part of the homeowner association (HOA) dues.

Visualize what your retirement life will entail. Decide where you want to live and what lifestyle you want. It is much easier if you start planning early rather than leaving it until to your last day of work.

When you are making decisions about retirement, you and your partner or spouse need to get on the same page. It is surprising to me how many couples have not talked about what they want to do in retirement. Where do you want to live? How do you want to spend your time? Do you want to ski or be near the beach? I have worked with couples who are not on the same page and do not want to talk about it for fear it will turn into a fight. I say better a fight now than a divorce later.

Marriage often means compromising to come to an agreement, and so does retirement. You have to talk about what your plans are. Do you want to live near the grandchildren or are you okay with living away and visiting? Do you want more than one home and to be snowbirds or do you plan to move to a sunnier climate? What amenities do you want your home to have? Do you plan to travel? Lifestyle questions are crucial for boomers to answer so they can plan their future, yet it is probably the most-unexamined topic in their marriages. Take a weekend to get away, spend time with each other and talk.

If you are single, you have the same thinking and decision-making to do. Where will you live? What is the lifestyle you want? Take some time to really think about what you want to do on a daily basis, and where you want to do it. If you want a second home, buying it before you quit work is a good idea so you can qualify for a mortgage. It is also good to consider applying for a home equity line of credit before you retire so you have it in case of an emergency. It is much easier to get a loan while you are employed than after you retire, so plan ahead.

I know from firsthand experience that unexpected death happens. Be sure your wills and life insurance policies are up to date. It is a good idea to review your wills after major life events like marriage, divorce, the birth of a new baby or grandchild, a major change in the tax law, the sale of a business, a change in health, or an inheritance.

Cross-generational Wealth-building Strategies

Every generation today is stuck in the wealth gap, where money is lacking. While the reasons and consequences vary, no one, no matter what their age, has escaped the consequences of a world that does not teach us how to manage money, invest well or get wealthy.

Compounding becomes the key for you. It is more important than ever to get good rates of return on your investments. I think having crypto as a 5% allocation in your portfolio is enough to make a *huge* difference. Refer back to the illustration where $1,000 invested in three different cryptos grew to over six figures in five years. Imagine that happens again with money invested in the right cryptocurrencies. Compounding your money becomes a little bit easier in a fast-growing, revolutionary asset class like cryptocurrencies, than it does earning a 10% average return in the stock market.

I truly think investing in cryptocurrencies is going to be a game changer for all generations. They are easy to invest in, no brokerage or advisor necessary; just do your research (like reading this book) and determine which cryptocurrencies you want to invest in. The nice thing is cryptocurrencies don't require a lot of money or additional investments like a 401(k).

And here is the icing on the cake. With only 10% of older people and 14% of all ages being invested, we are investing before the big wave of money comes in. I believe that a few years from now, cryptocurrencies will be integrated into all business and commerce. Looking back in five years, the returns will look spectacular and investors will start pouring in. Eventually, we will experience a frothy market in cryptocurrencies like the peak of Internet stocks as people understand what they are and salivate over the five and 10 years of past returns. This will probably happen around 2026, so we have an estimated five years before we are close to a peak.

The Bottom Line

While each generation has its own challenges and perspectives, the *Wealth Building Formula* applies to all. You may have less time or money, but the great equalizer is compounding. You need to take advantage of the cycle we are in no matter what your age and invest in cryptocurrency.

Leap into the Quantum Age

As a millennial, GenXer or baby boomer, write down your philosophies about wealth-building. What has you most concerned and most excited?

Chapter 18
How to Embrace Wealth in All Ways

"Use money for good and it will be good to you."

Wealth gives you freedom — the freedom to live comfortably, have time to do what you want, delegate work to others, share your good fortune and self-actualize by living your purpose. You might think of wealth as a way to own a nice car or several homes, or to travel. Of course, these things are possible with wealth, but those are more of a representation of what you expect wealth to be, rather than the reality of wealth.

When you are living with wealth and have wealth, it goes beyond "things." You can afford to take better care of your health, buy organic foods, pay for a personal trainer, take good vitamins and supplements, and see healthcare professionals (including masseuses, spas and other forms of holistic health).

One of the biggest uses of money is to create the environment you want. If you want to live in a tropical place, you can. If you want to live in the mountains, you can. If you want to fly private, you can. If you want to entertain your friends or family, or for charitable causes, you can. You can hire people to do it for you and take care of things for you. Delegating work to other people is a big benefit of having wealth. It frees up your time to do what you want to, whether that is golfing, shopping, traveling, painting; whatever you like.

It is up to you to live your life's purpose and feel satisfied that you are doing what you are here for. Being at peace with your soul and your creator go far beyond money. We can get fixated on money, but the reality is there are far more important things we are here for.

Money can provide ease in life and even relaxation, but you still have limited time on this planet. No amount of money can give you more than 24 hours a day. I am sure many billionaires would be happy to trade billions of dollars for more years to live, but we don't have that choice. Having good health is a major priority, and health is wealth. The ability to enjoy longevity and have energy, vitality and youthfulness has tremendous value.

Millionaires have some rich habits in common, according to Tom Corley, who wrote *Change Your Habits, Change Your Life* after studying self-made millionaires. He determined that over 80% of millionaires spent 60 minutes a day to dream. He called it "dream-setting" because it involved dreaming and goal-setting. It involved things outside of work, such as a side hustle or creating additional streams of income. When was the last time you did some dreaming and goal-setting? About 80% of millionaires also spend 60 minutes a day in some form of additional education, whether it was for their career, skill or industry. They studied to learn and improve themselves every day.

Peace of mind is also a form of wealth. Not worrying about how to pay for things, your ability to cover unforeseen expenses or helping others in need are things that money can do to help you relax. You won't have to worry about your kids as much if you can afford to provide a safe place for them to live. You can afford their educational expenses or any unforeseen medical expenses needed. Helping their family is something almost everyone I work with tells me they want to do.

If you are smart with your money, it can develop into generational wealth. You can leave money to future generations to pay for their homes or education. I don't recommend giving young people enough money to live a life of leisure, because that is a sure way to stunt their growth in life. It is good for people to learn things, strive to meet goals and get out of their comfort zones. However, helping with big-ticket items can be useful. I recommend giving kids or grandkids just enough help (for example, the down payment on a house) without spoiling them or stopping them from important self-development.

Money also lets you contribute to society and charities. Whatever causes are close to your heart, you can afford to help. Contributing money to charities always seems to come back to me, so I am a believer that if you support good causes, the money you give them will return in multiples. You also have the opportunity through charity to create a legacy, whether it is supporting humanitarian causes, making the planet a better place or improving the environment. Leaving money will make a difference where it is important to you and your values. Use money for good, and it will be good to you.

In the Time of the Pandemic

Before the pandemic, you might have felt pretty good about reaching your financial goals. You were working hard and saving for retirement, paying off debt, investing money, going on vacation and more. But then everything stopped. Nothing was certain anymore. We have all been affected, some much more than others. No one I know is sleeping well.

You might be looking around, trying to get your bearings and figuring out what to do next. You may be wondering what moves you can make that will help you be smart with your investments and improve your finances. Some people have moved out of large cities. Others are able to work from home for a short period of time. Still others are feathering their nests, remodeling and creating home offices. Our time horizon seems to have changed from a long-term perspective to "let's live life today."

People are making different financial decisions than they were six months or one year ago. You might be thinking more about your health, lifestyle, housing, vacation travel and what is best for your children. It can be very stressful. Everyone wants to tell you what to do. You might decide to spend money differently than you would have a year ago. It is okay to change your mind. It is okay to feel like you are living more for today. It is okay to do what makes you happy.

Take a deep breath. Stop and listen to your inner voice. This is your life and these are your decisions. Right now, joy is in short supply, so whatever you can do to increase your joy, do it.

Cut yourself some slack and allow yourself a little wiggle room to be happier. If you have been wanting to go to the beach or mountains, go. If you want to spruce up a room in your home, do it. If you want to spend money in a way you normally wouldn't, go ahead. There are times to allow yourself more flexibility with your finances and now is one of those times.

You can always get more money, but you can never buy more years.

Final Thoughts

I have shown you why now is a unique time in history to build wealth — how it is possible to literally save decades of time that it would normally take you to accumulate wealth. I have shown you why to invest, how to survive volatility and which cryptocurrencies to invest in.

Only you can take the information given and decide to do something with it. I am always amazed by people who pray for improved finances and when the answer appears, they ignore it. I believe this book is the answer you have been looking for.

If you are confused, look at it as a beginning point and get more information. If you are fearful, start small and work on your inner beliefs. If you are skeptical, do your research. The information is there, but it is not on your nightly news or in *Money* magazine. Look in the Additional Resources section of this book for where to get more information.

The Bottom Line

Wealth buys you freedom to do so many things for yourself, your family and your community. But it only comes from action. You are fortunate to be learning this years ahead of the crowd. Don't miss this opportunity.

Leap into the Quantum Age

Some people continuously research and never act. They buy courses, attend seminars, read books and never act. Even if you take only $100 and buy XRP, at least you are taking some action. That is much better than doing nothing or staying in "stuck" energy mode.

Already $2 trillion of new wealth has been created by cryptocurrencies. I believe that is a drop in the bucket of what is coming. The earlier you invest, the less risk you are taking. The longer you wait to invest, the more risk you are taking because the market value will be higher. Invest a little even if you are still doubtful. If you wait until you see it all play out, you will be too late. Grab your phone, download the Uphold app from the app store, connect your bank account and get started!

Additional Resources

How to Learn More about Cryptocurrency

To learn about cryptocurrency, there are many free podcasts available, including *Be Wealthy & Smart* on Apple Podcasts. All 950 of my podcast episodes are at *https://LindaPJones.com/podcasts.*

I recommend you go to my website and listen to my podcasts and interviews on my specially chosen cryptocurrency playlist at: *https://LindaPJones.com/podcast-list-cryptocurrencies/.*

Watch my free webinar ($1,500 value): "Financial Freedom by Investing in Cryptocurrencies" at *https://LindaPJones.com/bookbonus.* On the webinar you will learn:

- The wealth building potential of the 8 cryptocurrencies mentioned in the book
- Why they will experience exponential growth
- Strategies for accumulation

How to Connect with Linda

Sign up for the free newsletter on my website at *https://LindaPJones.com.*

Connect with me on Twitter *at https://Twitter.com/LindaPJones,*

Facebook at *https://Facebook.com/LindaPJonesFanPage* and

Instagram at *https://Instagram.com/LindaPJones.*

Other Books by Linda P. Jones

If you want more financial tips, your "Millionaire Action Plan" and/or a valuable checklist of financial action steps, I recommend you read my book, *You're Already a Wealth Heiress, Now Think and Act Like One, 6 Practical Steps for Making It a Reality Now!* It was just added to the list of "All Time Best Wealth Books" by BookAuthority for the third consecutive year.

It is available at bookstores and on Amazon.com, and internationally on Amazon.co.UK. This is my way of empowering women (and smart men) worldwide to financial freedom. (Yes, men love the book, too.)

How to Join Linda's VIP Investing Group

Stocks and cryptocurrencies are changing rapidly in the Quantum Age and it is important to stay up on what is happening, especially with investment opportunities, dominant technologies, regulations, trends and cycles. If you want to get your money working harder for you, learn what to invest in, and have a wealth mentor so you can gain confidence and financial freedom, consider joining the *Be Wealthy & Smart VIP Experience*, my private investing group. Because you have read this book, you are entitled to a 50% savings. Just use promo code **"SAVE50" at checkout.** For more information about the *Be Wealthy & Smart VIP Experience*, go to *https://lindapjones.com/why-join-the-vip-experience/.*

Key Word Glossary

Airdrop: A deposit of a start-up cryptocurrency into your crypto account or wallet, usually for free.

Alt Coins: Any cryptocurrency other than bitcoin.

AML: Anti-money laundering rules help detect and report suspicious financial activities, such as money laundering and terrorist financing.

Bitcoin: The first cryptocurrency was bitcoin (trading symbol is BTC). Satoshi Nakamoto is the name used by the presumed pseudonymous person or persons who developed bitcoin. He created a white paper that explained the technology and purpose of BTC. It began the concept of decentralized finance, or DeFi, which is a trustless financial network developed on blockchain protocol.

Blockchain: A secure record of transactions or blocks. It is essentially a digital ledger of transactions that is duplicated and distributed across the entire network of computer systems.

Compounding: Earning interest on principal and interest so money grows over time.

Cold Storage: Offline storage of crypto, such as on a thumb drive-like device called a Ledger Nano.

Cycle: An event that repeats at regular intervals so it may be projected into the future and add predictability.

Cryptocurrencies: A cryptocurrency (or crypto currency) is a digital asset designed to work as a medium of exchange that uses strong cryptography to secure financial transactions, control the creation of additional units and verify the transfer of assets operating in the network. Cryptocurrencies are not controlled outside the network and are decentralized, as opposed to traditional centralized central banking systems such as fiat currencies.

Decentralized Finance (DeFi): The decentralized financial services built on top of distributed blockchain networks with no central intermediaries such as banks, custodians and exchanges.

Deflationary currency: A cryptocurrency that is destroyed over time so less is in existence in the future; the opposite of an inflationary fiat currency.

Diamond hands: Refusing to sell for any reason; holding onto an investment in spite of volatility.

Digital asset: A non-physical asset that exists digitally, such as a cryptocurrency or non-fungible token.

Digital wallet: An online storage account for cryptocurrencies where cryptos are held.

Dogecoin or Doge: "The people's cryptocurrency." A crypto that is accepted by businesses as money. Also known as a "meme crypto" because it was associated with a popular meme of a Shiba Inu dog. Said to be invented by an IBM programmer as a joke, but adopted by Elon Musk as a favorite crypto.

Equities: Stocks; public ownership of a corporation that is traded on stock exchanges.

Fiat currency: A currency that has no physical asset backing the value. It relies on faith and confidence, and possibly a strong military, for people to use it. Cycle lasts 94 years.

Flare: As in Flare Network, a talented group of computer programmers who are creating smart contract capabilities for certain cryptocurrencies by adding the Flare Spark (trading symbol FLR) to XRP, XLM, Dogecoin, Litecoin, etc.

FUD: "Fear, Uncertainty and Doubt" created by media or pundits; sometimes used to manipulate investors to sell.

HODL: "Hold On for Dear Life" — means don't sell!

KYC: "Know Your Customer" — a banking law that says you must gather basic information to know who your customer is to prevent criminal activities.

Ledger Nano: A technology hardware/device that is purchased separately and is used to store crypto offline, not connected to the Internet.

Mint: Minting the computer process of validating information, creating a new block and recording that information in the blockchain.

Moon: A big move upward, gaining great value. "When Moon?"

Money engine: An investment that grows and compounds money, such as stocks, bonds, real estate, cryptocurrencies, businesses, etc.

Non-fungible tokens (NFTs): Unique works that are digital and can be purchased by others, such as a piece of art, song, music album, first tweet of Jack Dorsey, contract, license or deed.

Quantum Age: The technology revolution that comes after the creation of online communication and commerce. It is also called Web 3.0, the Internet of Value and the Fourth Industrial Revolution. Many new technologies will emerge, including but not limited to cryptocurrencies and digital assets.

Ripple (Ripple Labs, Inc.): An American technology company that developed the Ripple Ledger payment protocol and exchange network.

Securities: Tradable financial assets like stocks, which are equity securities, and bonds, which are debt securities.

Smart contract: A computer protocol intended to facilitate, verify or enforce a contract on the blockchain without third parties.

Stablecoin: A new class of cryptocurrencies that attempts to offer price stability and is backed by a reserve asset.

Tokenization (Tokenizing an asset): Issuing a digital token on a blockchain, where that token represents an underlying tangible or intangible asset.

Trustless: Transacting with one another in a "peer-to-peer" manner over the Internet. When you transfer value digitally from one account to another on the blockchain, you are trusting the underlying blockchain system to both enable that transfer and ensure sender authenticity and currency validity.

Unbanked: People without a banking relationship who can use cryptocurrencies to send and receive money via apps on their phones.

Valuation: The value of something. A market valuation is the amount of shares times the price per share. For example, the market valuation of all cryptocurrencies is $2 trillion.

XLM: Stellar Lumens (trading symbol is XLM) — a cryptocurrency that can act as a bridge, enabling users to trade between multiple currencies. Considered as money for the unbanked or people without a banking relationship.

XRP: Ripple Labs, Inc.'s bridge cryptocurrency, created for banks and cross-border payment networks as a means of payment settlement, a money transfer system, and currency exchange.

Disclaimer

make any claims whatsoever regarding past or future performance.

While the information herein has been obtained from publicly available sources that the firm believes to be reliable, the firm cannot and does not guarantee the accuracy, adequacy or completeness of any such information. The information herein may change from time to time without notice, and the firm has no obligation to update this material. The firm does not provide tax or legal advice. To the extent that any material herein concerns tax or legal matters, such information is not intended to be solely relied upon nor used for the purpose of making tax and/or legal decisions without first seeking independent advice from a tax and/or legal professional.

Full disclosure: I own all of the cryptocurrencies mentioned favorably in the book and stock in Ripple Labs, Inc.

About the Author

Linda P. Jones is America's Wealth Mentor™. She graduated from the University of Washington with a B.A. in Business and her career spanned over 25 years working for Wall Street firms. After her husband passed away suddenly from a brain aneurysm, she made it her life's mission to teach women (and smart men) to invest so they could achieve financial freedom.

Linda's first book, *You're Already a Wealth Heiress, Now Think and Act Like One: 6 Practical Steps to Make It a Reality Now!* is on the list of "All Time Best Wealth Books" by BookAuthority. Her award-winning podcast, *Be Wealthy & Smart,* is listened to in over 130 countries and has over 7 million downloads.

Linda shares wealth building secrets, tips, and knowledge that made her $2 million at age 39. She teaches that financial freedom is about making the right choices and investing well and believes anyone can become wealthy, no matter how much or how little money they are starting with.

Made in the USA
Middletown, DE
06 February 2022

60568389R00126